CW01333034

Don Bosco Publications

Vera Schauber / Michael Schindler

101 Saints
and Special People

Don Bosco Publications

© 2003 Don Bosco Publications
Reprinted 2011
Cover and layout: Margret Russer
Illustrations: Martina Spinková
Design : Don Bosco Graphic House Ensdorf,
Printed in the Czech Republic

ISBN 0-9544539-1-3

CONTENTS

Introduction 7

The Three Kings (6. 1.)	
Casper, Melchior, Balthasar 10
Sebastian (20. 1.) 12
Agnes of Rome (21. 1.) 13
Timothy (26. 1.) 14
Angela Merici (27. 1.) 15
John Bosco (31. 1.) 16
Blaise (3. 2.) 18
Veronica (4. 2.) 19
Dorothy (6. 2.) 20
Valentine (14. 2.) 21
Cyril and Methodius (14. 2.) 22
Matthias (24. 2.) 24
Casimir (4. 3.) 25
John of God (8. 3.) 26
Frances of Rome (9. 3.) 27
Patrick (17. 3.) 28
Joseph (19. 3.) 30
Benjamin (31. 3.) 32
Bernadette (16. 4.) 33
Conrad (21. 4.) 34
Adalbert (23. 4.) 35
George (23. 4.) 36
Mark (25. 4.) 37
Catherine of Sienna (29. 4.) 38
Phillip and James (3. 5.) 40
Alexander (3. 5.) 41
Florian (4. 5.) 42
Sophie (15. 5.) 43
John Nepomucene (16. 5.) 44
Felix (18. 5.) 46
Rita (22. 5.) 47
Julia (22. 5.) 48
Philip Neri (26. 5.) 49

Joan of Arc (30. 5.) 50
Boniface (5. 6.) 52
Anthony of Padua (13. 6.) 54
John the Baptist (24. 6.) 56
Peter and Paul (29. 6.) 58
Thomas (3. 7.) 60
Ulric (4. 7.) 61
Benedict (11. 7.) 62
Henry and Cunegundes (13. 7.) 64
Margaret (20. 7.) 65
Daniel (21. 7.) 66
Mary Magdalene (22. 7.) 68
Bridget (23. 7.) 70
Christopher (24. 7.) 71
Christina (24. 7.) 72
James the Great (25. 7.) 73
Anne and Joachim (26. 7.) 74
Ignatius of Loyola (31. 7.) 76
Dominic (8. 8.) 78
Laurence (10. 8.) 79
Clare of Assisi (11. 8.) 80
Maximilian Kolbe (14. 8.) 82
Bernard of Clairvaux (20. 8.) 84
Bartholomew (24. 8.) 85
Louis (25. 8.) 86
Augustine (28. 8.) 87
Mary (8. 9.) 88
Robert Bellarmine (17. 9.) 90
Hildegard (17. 9.) 91
Stanislaus (18. 9.) 92
Matthew (21. 9.) 94
Jonah (21. 9.) 95
Cosmas and Damian (26. 9.) 96
Vincent de Paul (27. 9.) 97

Wenceslaus (28. 9.)	98
Michael (29. 9.)	100
Gabriel (29. 9.)	101
Raphael (29. 9.)	102
Theresa of Lisieux (1. 10.)	103
Francis of Assisi (4. 10.)	104
Faustina Kowalska (5. 10.)	106
Sarah (9. 10.)	107
Denis (9. 10.)	108
Teresa of Avila (15. 10.)	110
Luke (18. 10.)	111
Ursula (21. 10.)	112
Simon (28. 10.)	113
Charles Borromeo (4. 11.)	114
Leonard (6. 11.)	115
Martin (11. 11.)	116
Elizabeth of Hungary (19. 11.)	118
Cecilia (22. 11.)	120
Andrew (30. 11.)	121
Francis Xavier (3. 12.)	122
Barbara (4. 12.)	123
Nicholas (6. 12.)	124
Lucy (13. 12.)	126
Stephen (26. 12.)	127
John the Apostle (27. 12.)	128
David (29. 12.)	129
Sylvester (31. 12.)	130

Saints and Special People in Alphabetical Order 132

My Name 137

INTRODUCTION

Why are you called Luke? Why is she called Ann? Some day a person may wonder why they have a particular name. My name is important, a human being without a name is not a complete person. It is always interesting to know the story behind a name, why one child is called Patrick and another Veronica. Was it because the parents admired a certain actor or athlete? Or are they passing on the name of a grandparent or another member of the family? Or is there some other reason why are we are called by the names we have? We would all like to know.

What does your name actually mean? Which country did it come from? Who is the person hiding behind your name. What did they do? How did they live? Why did their name become so popular? Who was that person whose name is now my name? Looking for that person is always interesting.

Often we have to go back many centuries in history to find that person. The lives of some are preserved in legends or stories, rich in significance to remind us of the quality of their lives. For others we have just vague details. While for some, who lived nearer to our time, we have exact information and many details of their lives. What we do know is, that everyone of them made a great impression on the people of their day. They left us more than their name, they left us their life inspiration. They are all remembered for different reasons, some like St John Bosco devoted their lives to caring for poor children. Others, like St Francis of Assisi, gave up their wealth to devote their lives to looking after the poor. Some saints were educators, some were parents, some were martyrs, some were popes, some bishops, some simply ordinary Christians.

Whoever they were, whatever work they did, they cannot be forgotten, their name keeps them alive in our memory. It would be a great pity if all we knew about them was their name. Across the 2000 years since the birth of Christ there have been so many saints right up to our own time. Every age produces its own saints. Recently we have been blessed with the life and outstanding work of Mother Teresa, everyone remembers all the great work she did for sick and destitute people. Although she died in recent times, she is as much a saint as Saint Barbara or Saint Martin.

But what exactly is a saint? How does one become a saint? If you were able to ask the question of any one of the women or men described in this book, they would not know the answer. Not one of them would have thought they were a saint. Without any fuss they were just living out their normal life. But suddenly something happened. It is difficult to put it into words, because it happened in a different way with every saint. All we can say is, that God stepped into their lives. And these people sensed that they could trust Him. He took them by the hand and showed them the way. They felt securely rooted in God, as a tree, whose roots are deep in the earth. They felt as secure as a tree that no strong wind can tear from the ground. And because they had experienced God's love for them, they each tried, in their own way, to show this love to others. They were not always strong heroes or brave women. Many knew dark days in their lives, when they felt like despairing of their ability to live up to their ideals. Nevertheless they tried, again and again, to work for God and his people. Some of them seemed to fail miserably at first.

They suffered loneliness, hostilities and even paid the price of their convictions by death. However, their death became for many people quite an important sign. The mighty oppressors of this world tried to destroy them, but they could not destroy the love these people had for each other. Saints are important to us. They are like coloured windows, through which the light of the sun shines. One cannot look directly at the sun, because the light is too strong. But the sun seems to give life to the colours in a window. So we feel, through the lives of the saints, the warmth of God's love for us. Today there are still these special girls and boys, women and men. All over the world they live out their inspirational lives. They live in the hope of forming a better world. They are to be found where so many people do not want to be, with the poorest of street children, with lonely people who are dying, nursing the sick who have no one to care for them. And what is so special about them is that they have found great happiness in what they do. The example of their lives inspires others to join them. I'm sure that those who read this book will sense something of the impression the lives of the these saints and special people made on those that knew them.

In this book Vera Schauber and Michael Schindler tell the lives of the saints and special people in such an interesting and exciting way. Martina Spinková, an accomplished artist from the Czech republic, has painted pictures to match the lives. Each picture is alive with meaning, there is so much to discover in each one of them. Although most of the people we meet in this book came from Europe, they are known throughout the world. I first became aware of these special people when I was a child in Mexico, their lives were an inspiration to me then. Today, as I travel round the world, I meet people who proudly bear names similar to the people in this book. Reading their lives is a voyage of discovery. I'm sure you will enjoy the journey.

Pascual Chávez Villanueva,
Rector Major of the Salesians of Don Bosco

101 Saints
and Special People

The Three Kings

6 January

The legend of the three kings, or the three wise men, as part of the Christmas story is known throughout the world. They are often called the three wise men because they were so learned, but in some countries they are called magicians or wizards.

The three friendly kings, Casper, Melchior and Balthasar, heard that a mighty king had been born near Jerusalem. They decided to find him and honour him with gifts of gold, frankincense and myrrh. Carefully, they loaded their camels and elephants and started the long and arduous journey through the desert.

They travelled mostly at night to avoid the heat of the day. After many days they were lost, they no longer knew which way to go. Suddenly, looking up, they saw a star. The star shone brighter than anything else in the clear night sky. It seemed to say, 'Follow me!'

With faith they continued their journey, following the star.

Casper, Melchior and Balthasar

As they neared Jerusalem they thought that this was where the great king would be born, but the star continued its journey across the sky. It passed many grand houses in Jerusalem and the palace of the wicked King Herod. Finally, it came to rest above a dimly lit stable in a little town called Bethlehem. There, amongst the animals, the three kings saw Mary and Joseph and the baby Jesus. They had expected a great king in a beautiful palace, but they found instead, in this lowly stable, a tiny baby who would save the world.

Full of pride, the three kings made their way home. When they arrived in their own countries they had so much to tell their subjects. They told them of a new king who had been born in Bethlehem, to whom they had presented their gifts. On the 6th January each year the visit of the three kings is remembered and celebrated. It is called the feast of the Epiphany.

> The wise men expected to find a great king in a palace but found a tiny baby born in a stable. Why do you think God sent his son to be born in this way and not surrounded by riches?

Jesper, Jasper, Caspar, Gaspar, Kasper

Melcher

Balthazar, Balthes, Balz, Balzer

20 JANUARY

SEBASTIAN

Sebastian is known as the patron saint of the sick, because he survived terrible injuries and became well again. He was a Roman soldier and was also a Christian. The Emperor of Rome, at that time, was a man called Diocletian, who did not believe in Christ. He worshipped a Roman god and cruelly persecuted the Christians. However, Sebastian was a good soldier and Diocletian liked him. He tried to ignore the fact he was a very prayerful person, who often took food to Christians who were in prison.

In time, Sebastian converted more and more people to Christianity. This tried the patience of the Emperor Diocletian. When he heard that Sebastian had even converted to Christianity a very important judge in the city, he thought that it was time to act. He ordered Sebastian to be killed. Sebastian was tied to a post and shot with arrows until they thought he was dead.

As he lay lifeless on the ground, a Christian woman called Irene, asked if she could bury his body. She soon discovered, that although he was badly injured, he was still alive. Slowly and lovingly she nursed him back to health.

Having survived this terrible ordeal he bravely returned to Diocletian, who was furious that Sebastian was still alive. In front of everyone, Sebastian called Diocletian a persecutor of Christians. This enraged Diocletian even further and once more he condemned Sebastian to death. This time he succeeded and Sebastian was beaten to death in Rome on 20th January in the year 288 AD.

Sebastian found the courage to challenge cruelty. How can the cruelty in today's world be challenged?

Bastian, Bastien, Bastin, Seb, Sebastiano, Sébastien, Sebesta

AGNES OF ROME

21 JANUARY

The name Agnes means lamb. This was an appropriate name for Agnes, as she was a kind and gentle person, as gentle as a lamb. Agnes was a very beautiful girl and was admired by everyone, but from a very early age she had decided never to marry. She wanted to devote her life to Christ.

However, in about the year 304 AD, a young man called Claudius fell in love with Agnes and wanted her as his wife. But Agnes rejected him. The father of Claudius was a very powerful man, and when he heard about the rejection of his son, he was furious. He ordered that Agnes should be captured and imprisoned.

Claudius visited Agnes in her cell. He wanted to harm her. But before he could get close to her, he collapsed and died. Agnes prayed over the body of Claudius and miraculously he came back to life. Instead of being grateful to Agnes, the father of Claudius condemned her to death. He was suspicious of her and decided she would be burned as a witch.

Crowds gathered to watch. Agnes did not cry, or beg for her life, she remained quiet and put her trust in Jesus. As the fire was lit she was as dignified and gentle as ever. Suddenly, to the astonishment of the crowds, the flames mysteriously went out. This made the father of Claudius even angrier. He ordered her to be killed with a sword. Bravely, Agnes died as a martyr.

Agnes is honoured as the patron saint of brides. On 21st of January each year, there is a beautiful tradition, which takes place in the Church of St Agnes in Rome. Two small lambs are blessed in memory of the life of this brave and gentle girl.

Agnes decided to put God first in her life. How can you put God into your life?

Aggie, Aggy, Agna, Agnesa, Agnese, Agneta, Agnita, Ines, Nesa

26 JANUARY

TIMOTHY

Timothy was the trusted friend and helper of Paul the apostle. They met when Paul was visiting Lystra in Lycaonia. This was in the Province of Galatia, which today is part of Turkey. Timothy lived there with his family. His mother Eunice and grandmother Lois had been baptised by Paul and had become Christians.

Later when Paul returned once more to Lystra, Timothy asked if he could help him in his work, spreading Christ's message. Paul thought Timothy was very young for such a responsible job, but he liked and trusted him.

He needed someone to share his heavy workload on his long and exhausting missions. He agreed to let Timothy accompany him on his journey, taking the Christian faith to the rest of the world. Paul often reminded him, "Don't let people ignore you because you're young. If you are a good example, in the way you behave and the way you speak, they will know you are a good Christian."

Timothy travelled far and wide helping Paul in his missionary work. Together they led thousands of people towards a knowledge and understanding of Christ. Paul always acknowledged Timothy's hard work and dedication.

Many years later Timothy became Bishop of the Christian community in Ephesus. He was a holy and devout man, and remained there long after the death of Paul. He was admired and respected by the people, and finally died at a great age in the year 97 AD.

? Timothy was young, but he gave a good example to others. Who do you know who gives you a good example?

Tim, Timmie, Timmo, Timmy, Timo, Timoteo

14

ANGELA MERICI

27 JANUARY

In 1484, when Angela Merici was ten years old, her parents died. Angela went to live with her uncle and didn't return to her hometown of Brescia, in Italy, until after his death. She had grown into a wise and caring person. She had taught herself many things and had become aware of the needs of others. Many women in the town recognised her ability to listen and to advise, and would often turn to her in times of trouble.

At that time, girls from poorer families had little or no education. Angela knew that to help them and to give them hope for the future, she had to teach them herself. As more and more girls wanted to learn, she enlisted the help of unmarried women friends. Inspired by Angela, they taught the girls with the same love and dedication. News of the way they educated girls impressed many people and they were asked to bring their teaching skills to other towns.

These women formed themselves into a religious community and took St Ursula as their patron saint. For many years Angela and her helpers worked tirelessly, educating girls from poorer families, and giving them a love of God. Angela's work spread far and wide. She died on 27th January 1540.

The Ursulines were the first religious order of women devoted to teaching. Many girls, all over the world, owe their education to the Ursulines and their founder Angela Merici.

Angela was a wise and caring person. Who do you know who has these qualities?

Angel, Angelica, Angelina, Angelique, Angell, Angelo, Angie

John Bosco

John Bosco was born on 16th August 1815, the son of a poor farmer, in a little village in Italy called Becchi. From a very early age John wanted to become a priest. Although he faced many obstacles during his studies, he was finally ordained on 5th June 1841. He was called Don Bosco, which means Father Bosco in Italian. After his ordination to the priesthood, he began working in the city of Turin. He was shocked when he saw how many children had no homes.

When he offered to help one young boy, six friends came with him. Gradually, numbers grew and more homeless children arrived. Don Bosco played football with them, and cooked for them. He taught them skills such as carpentry and tailoring, and gave them hope for the future. Later he built orphanages and provided the boys with a home. He soon realised he could not do this by himself. In 1859 he founded a religious order, which is now known as the Salesians of Don Bosco.

Some areas of Turin, at this time, were dangerous. Whenever Don Bosco was threatened, a large grey dog, called Grigio, mysteriously appeared to protect him. His mother, Mama Margaret, who supported him in his work, constantly worried about him. He worked long and hard, and was often sick. Some local people resented him. They considered the boys were more trouble than they were worth. However, many valued the great work he was doing.

Don Bosco heard of a group of young women, led by Mary Mazzarello, who were working with young people. He encouraged them to become Sisters and do the same work for girls, as he and the other priests were doing for the boys. He told them,
"Always live in the presence of God.
Be gentle, patient and kind.
Help your girls to love God with all their hearts."
Mary Mazzarello and her sisters worked very hard for the girls. They became known as The Salesian Sisters. Some years after she died, she was declared a saint.

When Don Bosco died on 31st January 1888, the streets of Turin were lined with thousands of mourners. Today the work of Don Bosco has spread. Members of the Salesian Family continue to educate and care for young people throughout the world.

John Bosco and his fellow Salesians provided an education for the children with no hope for the future. How can education provide a better future for today's children?

Bosco, Eoin, Evan, Gianni, Giovanni, Hans, Hanke, Hanko, Hannemann, Hannes, Hans, Iaian, Ian, Ivan, Iven, Iwan, Jack, Jan, Jannis, Jean, Johann, Juan, Nino, Seain, Sean, Shane, Shawn, Zane

3 FEBRUARY

BLAISE

Blaise is the patron saint of those with illnesses of the throat. He was a doctor who cared deeply for the people he treated. He was also a committed Christian. At the beginning of the fourth century he was appointed Bishop of Sebaste, and worked tirelessly for the people of his diocese. It was a difficult time; Christians were still being persecuted by the Romans. Many were even killed because they refused to give up their belief in Jesus.

The enemies of the Christians often pursued Blaise. He sometimes fled into the forest to escape. There he lived in a cave and made friends with the animals. Birds would often bring him fruit and berries to eat. Injured animals, such as foxes, would come to him and he would lovingly tend their wounds.

Eventually Blaise was captured and imprisoned by his enemies. One day, a young boy in the same prison swallowed a fish bone. He was in danger of choking to death. Blaise prayed to God to save the boy. Suddenly the bone was dislodged from his throat and the boy recovered. The Romans saw this miracle as a sign that Blaise was becoming too powerful and he was condemned to death.

On 3rd February in many churches, all over the world, the miracle Blaise worked for the boy, is remembered. People come to church for the blessing of St Blaise. Crossed candles are placed under the chin, and across the throat. The priest then prays that, by the intercession of St Blaise, people may be freed from all ailments of the throat.

Blaise had the gift of healing that made others jealous. Are you jealous of other people's gifts?

Blase, Blasi, Blaze, Bliss

18

VERONICA

4 FEBRUARY

Many people are remembered for special events and actions which took place during their lifetime. However, when we think of Veronica, we recall something that happened for only a few moments. Veronica is remembered as the person who wiped the face of Jesus, as he made his journey to Calvary. It is said that the image of Christ's face remained on the cloth.

Veronica lived in Jerusalem, on the road that led to Calvary. On the day we now know as Good Friday, crowds had gathered along the side of the road. They had come to watch, as Jesus carried his cross on the painful journey towards his crucifixion. The enemies of Jesus had mixed with the crowd. They had started to shout and scream at him. Very soon, many in the crowd were doing the same. But some of the crowd were just standing there, watching silently, and feeling his pain. Many women were weeping. They were mothers, thinking of their own sons.

One of these women was Veronica. She watched as Jesus walked the dusty road. She saw the heavy cross on his shoulders and the pain in his eyes. Blood from the crown of thorns ran down his face. She had heard about his kindness and compassion towards the poor and suffering.

She knew he did not deserve to be crucified. Slowly she stepped forward. She took a clean cloth and gently wiped his face. In that moment she recognised his greatness. She realised he truly was the Son of God.

> Veronica showed kindness to Jesus when others were against him. How could you help when someone is being badly treated by other people?

Berenice, Berenike, Bernice, Beronica, Nica, Nicky, Ron, Ronnie, Vera, Verona, Veronia, Véronique

6 FEBRUARY

DOROTHY

Images of Dorothy always portray her as a beautiful young woman with a circle of flowers in her hair. She holds a basket of flowers and apples, and there is a smile on her face.

She lived with her parents and her two sisters in Cappadocia, in a country which is now known as Turkey. It was a difficult time for Dorothy's family. Like many Christians they were persecuted for their belief in Jesus. A judge in the city, a man called Fabricio, admired Dorothy and wanted her as his wife. He told her that he wanted to marry her. But he was not a Christian; they did not share the same beliefs. Dorothy refused to marry him. This filled Fabricio with rage. He locked Dorothy up in prison for nine days and nine nights without food. He hoped that ordeal might change her mind.

However, she came out of the prison healthy and even more beautiful than ever. Fabricio ranted with fury. Aware of how much Dorothy loved her two sisters, he had them burned at the stake. He warned Dorothy that if she still refused to marry him, she too would die this awful death. She said to him quietly,

"I am not afraid to die. On the contrary I am happy to be able to gather my roses and apples in the garden of Jesus Christ."

A lawyer, named Theophilus, made fun of her and asked her to send him some fruit from 'her garden' when she arrived in heaven. To his amazement, shortly after her death, an angel appeared and presented him with a basket containing three roses and three apples. When Theophilus saw the basket of flowers and fruit, he fell on the ground in fright. After seeing this miracle, he loudly declared his belief in Christ. Dorothy showed no fear as she went to her death in the fire. She died in the year 305 AD.

Dorothy kept calm and close to God when faced with angry people. Can you stay calm and close to God when people annoy you?

Dodo, Dolly, Dora, Doreen, Dorette, Doriet, Dorina, Dorinda, Doris, Dorita, Dorothea, Dorothee, Dorothée, Dot, Dottie, Thea, Theda

VALENTINE

14 FEBRUARY

Valentine is recognised throughout the world as the patron saint of people in love. Long ago it was thought that a girl would marry the first boy she saw on the morning of February 14th. This led to the tradition of a boy waiting outside the house of his sweetheart at dawn, so that he would be the first person the girl would see.

Valentine was the Bishop of Terni, a city in southern Italy. At that time it was difficult for Christians to openly state their belief in Jesus. Valentine was not discouraged. He often went out onto the streets preaching the Gospel, and telling people about Christ. He introduced the custom of gathering fresh flowers from his garden and presenting them to all young couples when they came to church.

One day, as the local men were preparing to go to war, he tried to persuade them not to fight, but to stay at home with their wives and families who loved them. News of this angered the Emperor who was leading the war. He feared that Valentine was causing unrest among his troops, and damaging the morale of his army.

He decided to solve the problem by having Valentine arrested and killed.

Now on 14th February Valentine is remembered and it is customary on that day to give cards and flowers to the one you love. In Dublin, there is a shrine dedicated to St Valentine. Many couples come to the Eucharistic celebration on his feast day, which also includes a Blessing of Rings for those about to be married. The shrine is also visited throughout the year by couples, who come to pray to St Valentine and to ask him to watch over them in their lives together.

❓ Valentine wanted to help young people who were in love. Which young couples would you pray for today?

Val, Valeda, Valente, Valentian, Valentin, Valentino, Valina, Valtin, Veltin

14 FEBRUARY

CYRIL AND

Cyril and Methodius were brothers from Thessolonica, Greece. They were born during the ninth century to a prominent Christian family. They were given an excellent education and were very hardworking students. Friends of Cyril even called him 'The Philosopher' because he was so knowledgeable.

Cyril and Methodius became priests, and were soon sent on a special mission to countries north of Greece. Although it was now over eight hundred years since the birth of Christ, many people in these countries were not yet Christians. The rulers needed Cyril and Methodius to spread Christ's message, and since they both spoke the language of the Slavic people, they were ideal for the task.

They were very enthusiastic about this challenge and worked tirelessly for many years. Cyril invented a special alphabet and with the help of Methodius used this to translate the Gospels and some liturgical books into the Slavonic language. Thus, the teachings of Jesus were in a language the people could understand. The people listened to the brothers and admired their dedication.

Although Cyril and Methodius converted thousands to Christianity they were not without their critics. Many thought that it was not right to translate the Church's liturgy into another language. News of this criticism reached the pope and he sent for the brothers. Much to everyone's surprise, the pope approved of their method of spreading Christ's message and they were named as bishops.

Unfortunately, Cyril died before he could be consecrated bishop, and Methodius lived another sixteen years and died in the year 869 AD. Although they both died over a thousand years ago, it was only recently they were given the title, Patrons of Europe. The brothers are still honoured today in Slavic countries, for bringing Christianity to the people.

Cyril and Methodius used their gift for languages to bring different people together. How do you treat people who are different?

Cyra, Cyrill, Cyrilla, Cyrille, Kirill, Kryil   Method, Metodio

22

METHODIUS

MATTHIAS

24 FEBRUARY

Matthias was not one of the original apostles selected by Jesus as his followers. He took the place of Judas, one of the original twelve apostles. Judas had betrayed Jesus in the garden of Gethsemane. He soon realised the awful thing he had done, but it was too late, the soldiers had taken Jesus away. Judas was filled with remorse and went to a nearby field, where he killed himself.

Jesus had chosen twelve apostles to represent the twelve tribes of Israel. The remaining apostles decided to choose another man to take the place of Judas. They could not decide between Joseph Barsabbas or Matthias, both were highly respected. They spent some time in prayer, asking for guidance. They then cast lots and Matthias won. Joseph Barsabbas happily accepted the decision. He knew Matthias was a good man and congratulated him.

Matthias was deeply moved by the death of Jesus and his resurrection. He felt privileged, as an apostle, to continue the work started by Jesus. He travelled far and wide as a missionary, moving from country to country, telling people about Jesus. He baptised many, converting thousands to Christianity.

However, not everyone listened to him. Some saw him as a threat to their own beliefs and wanted to hurt him. One day he was given a cup of poisoned wine to drink. Matthias quickly noticed this, but said nothing. He prayed quietly and then drank the cup of wine. Much to the astonishment of his enemies he survived. They were furious and threw stones at him. They did not stop until they were certain he was dead. Although he was not chosen by Jesus to be one of the original twelve, by his love and dedication to spreading the good news of Jesus, Matthias had proved himself a worthy apostle.

Matthias was the last apostle to be chosen and he felt welcomed by the others. Do you find it easy to welcome new people into your life?

Massey, Mateo, Mathe, Matheis, Mathis, Mats, Matt, Matteo, Mattheson, Mattheus, Matthe

CASIMIR

4 MARCH

Casimir was the son of a king. His father was King Casimir IV of Poland. His mother Queen Elizabeth came from Austria. He had twelve brothers and sisters and he was the third eldest. From a very early age it was obvious that he was not like the rest of the family. He was not interested in wealth and splendour, and would rather sleep on a hard floor than a soft bed. He was a very holy and devout person, and enjoyed visiting the little chapel in the palace.

As Casimir grew older he continued to reject his wealthy surroundings. He wanted to share the sufferings of the poor, and often gave them food. One of his father's servants seeing this, shook his head in disbelief. He said, "This is not the behaviour of a prince."
Casimir quietly told him, that in serving the poor, he was also serving Christ. The servant was ashamed and apologised to Casimir, and asked forgiveness for his harsh words.

Casimir was destined to become ruler of the neighbouring country, Hungary. To the astonishment of everyone he rejected this great honour. He never wanted to wear a crown; he only wanted to serve God. Although his parents were very surprised, they respected his decision and let him lead his own life.

Later Casimir became ill, and gradually became weaker and weaker. On 4th March 1484 at the very young age of twenty-five years he died, surrounded by his loving family. Although they mourned him they knew that at last he was at peace. He was with God.

Casimir chose a simple life without buying and owning lots of things. Would you find it difficult to live without some of your possessions?

Casimiro, Casmir, Kasmir, Kazamira

JOHN OF GOD

8 MARCH

John was born in Portugal in 1495. His family was poor. As a very young boy he packed his bag and ran away from home. He moved to Spain and worked as a shepherd for a while. When he was old enough he joined the Spanish army.

After his military service, he travelled around the towns and villages selling religious books and pictures. He made very little money, but as a devout person it was his way of spreading God's word.

One day, on his travels, he listened to a sermon given by John of Avila. This had a profound effect on him and he decided to make amends for any wrong he had done. He walked the streets praising God and preaching to anyone who would listen. People looked at him in horror. They thought he was mad, and he was quickly put into the Royal Hospital for the Insane. John's time in the hospital was difficult. He couldn't believe how badly the patients were treated. He decided to do all he could to improve the lives of the sick and homeless.

In 1539 he opened his first hospital. Life was not easy, but his work was admired and soon others followed his example, nursing the sick with care and devotion. They treated them with sensitivity and dignity, something they had never known before. Soon his work spread and similar hospitals opened all over Spain. The Bishop of Granada admired John's work with the sick. When he heard that John often gave his cloak away to the needy, he presented him with a special cloak to wear. This became the distinctive uniform, the habit of the religious order he founded, which is now called the Hospitaller Order of St John of God.

John died in 1550. The religious order he founded continues to care for the sick all over the world. He is honoured as the patron saint of the sick and those who care for them.

? John treated the sick with dignity. How do you respect the dignity of others?

Eoin, Evan, Gianni, Giovanni, Hans, Hanke, Hanko, Hannemann, Hannes, Hans, Iaian, Ian, Ivan, Iven, Iwan, Jack, Jan, Jannis, Jean, Johann, Juan, Nino, Seain, Sean, Shane, Shawn, Zane

Frances of Rome

9 MARCH

On 9th March in Rome, police cars, buses, ambulances and private cars assemble before the church of Santa Maria. There is a long tradition of drivers coming every year to receive the blessing of Saint Frances who is buried in the church. Frances of Rome is the patron of motorists. She may seem a strange choice of patron since Frances lived in the 15th Century, when there were no cars. There is a simple explanation: Frances had great devotion to her guardian angel, and motorists driving in the hectic traffic of Rome, know they really need a guardian angel to protect them.

Frances had to endure great sorrow in her life. Her entire family died in a civil war. Her beloved husband, Lorenzo, was taken away from her and imprisoned for several years. Shortly afterwards, her son Battista was also imprisoned. Later, her six-year-old daughter Agnes died of the plague. Finally, when her seven-year-old son Evangelista died, she almost lost the will to live. Frances would never have coped, if it had not been her belief that her guardian angel was at her side.

As a result of the war her house was in ruins. Her husband was gone, one son was dead, and one a hostage. However, Frances took great comfort in the knowledge, that God had given her a guardian angel for protection. There were others worse off than her. She knew she must carry on. Courageously, she cleared out the wreckage of her house, and turned it into a makeshift hospital and a shelter for the homeless. Then she walked the streets of Rome giving food to the poor.

In order to get more support for her work, Frances established a Christian community of women. When her husband Lorenzo was finally released from prison, Frances nursed him until he died. His last words to her were,

"I feel as if my whole life has been one beautiful dream of purest happiness. God has given me so much in your love."

Frances died, on 9th March 1440 and the whole of Rome mourned.

> Frances found an inner strength to carry on when things went wrong. Do you find it difficult to continue when things go wrong in your life?

Francesca, Francette, Francisca, Franciska, Francoise, Franeka, Fran, Franny, Frannie, Franzi

27

PATRICK

17 MARCH

Patrick's feast day is on 17th March. He is the patron saint of Ireland. His parents were Romans living in Scotland, and he was born there in the year 385 AD. When Patrick was about 15 years old, he was captured and taken as a slave to Ireland.

For many years he worked as a shepherd, looking after the sheep in the beautiful Irish countryside. Eventually, he managed to escape and returned to his family. He then moved to France and studied the Christian faith.

In France, Patrick became a monk and later, he was consecrated as a bishop. But during all this time he never forgot Ireland and its people. Eventually, he returned to Ireland to tell the people about Christ. Many had never heard about Jesus. They were mostly Druids and Pagans, and did not fully understand what he was telling them. Many objected to him, and wanted him to leave Ireland.

Gradually people began to understand. With the help of his loyal followers Patrick travelled all over Ireland. They baptised people and built little churches of wood and clay, so that the Christian people had somewhere to meet. Everywhere Patrick went people came to know and love Christ. He used the lowly shamrock, growing in Ireland's rich soil, to explain the Trinity to them.

Patrick died in Ireland on 17th March in the year 461 AD. His followers continued to spread God's message, not only across Ireland, but also to many parts of Europe.

The people never forgot Patrick, and his feast day is celebrated all over the world. On 17th March, people wear green, the colour of the fields where Patrick once worked as a young shepherd. They also wear small bunches of shamrock, as a reminder of the Trinity, the three persons in one God.

Patrick made a lasting impression on the people of Ireland, and they have never forgotten him. What kind of impression do you make on those around you?

Paddy, Pat, Patric, Patrice, Patricia, Patricius, Patrico, Patrik, Patriz, Patrizio, Patrizius, Patty, Padraic, Padraig, Rick, Ricky

19 MARCH

JOSEPH

Joseph is a very special saint. He was a carpenter in Nazareth and was engaged to Mary. When he heard that Mary was to give birth to a child who would be the Son of God, he was afraid. He did not understand.

One night an angel appeared to him and told him not to be afraid.
"Mary will have a son and he will be called Jesus."
Joseph realised he had been given a great honour. He knew at once what he must do. He would support Mary and love and care for her son as if he were his own.

As the time of the birth drew near, there was an official census. Everyone had to register in the place where they were born. Joseph was born in Bethlehem, and Mary and Joseph made the long and tiring journey to the little town. It was late when they arrived, and the town was full of people who had come for the census. At first Mary and Joseph could not find anywhere to stay. Finally, they found a kindly innkeeper. Joseph told him Mary was about to give birth and he let them stay in his stable.

That night, Jesus was born, and Mary laid him carefully in the manger. As Joseph looked at them he felt very protective. He knew the responsibility God had placed on him. He was determined to devote his life to caring for Mary and her newborn son Jesus. Eventually the family returned to Nazareth. Joseph worked as a carpenter, and as Jesus grew he enjoyed helping Joseph in his little workshop.
When Jesus was twelve years old the family travelled to Jerusalem for the feast of the Passover. Although the journey took three days, they were with many other people and the time passed quickly. On the first day of the return journey it was getting late and Mary could not find Jesus. She thought at first he was with Joseph, but as soon as she saw him she realised Joseph was alone. He told her he had not seen Jesus all day. He had assumed Jesus was with Mary. He said,
"Try not to upset yourself Mary, he's probably playing with the other children." They looked for him everywhere but they still could not find him. They were frantic with worry and decided to return to Jerusalem.

The city was busy as usual. The Passover celebrations were completed and people had returned to work. Together Joseph and Mary searched the streets and the market place, but he was nowhere to be found. Finally, they returned to the temple. To their great relief and amazement they saw him.

He was sitting with a small crowd of learned men. He was teaching them and telling them about God. They marvelled at his understanding of such matters. They could not understand how a young child could have such knowledge and wisdom.

Suddenly, Jesus saw Mary and Joseph. He saw how proudly they were looking at him, but he also saw the worry and concern in their faces. He was sorry he had caused them so much pain. He had enjoyed speaking to these learned men and hadn't realised how time had passed.

Joseph willingly accepted the great responsibility given to him by God. Do you find it difficult to accept responsibility?

Beppe, Beppo, Giuseppe, Joe, Joey, José, Josip, Jossif, Ossip, Pepe, Pepito, Peppino, Peppone, Yussuf, Josie, Iosef, Isoep, Josiah, Josias, Seosaidh

"I'm sorry, I thought you knew I would be in the temple," he said.

At first Mary and Joseph did not understand what he meant. Later they realised that the time would come when he would leave them to begin God's work.

Today St Joseph is revered as the protector of families, and is the patron saint of workers.

31 MARCH

BENJAMIN

Long before the birth of Jesus, there lived a woman called Rachel. She was the second wife of Jacob. He loved his wife very much but for many years they remained childless. Jacob's first wife Leah had given him six sons and a daughter, but Rachel longed to give her husband a child.

Some time passed and Rachel and Jacob eventually had their longed-for child. A son was born and he was named Joseph. Many years later Rachel found she was expecting a second child. Just before the birth Rachel sensed that all was not well.

She feared she would soon die. She was very frightened and did not expect to see her second child. However, they were overjoyed when the second child was born safely. They had been blessed with another son.

Soon after the birth, just as she feared, Rachel died. Jacob was heartbroken but he was determined to care for his son. He renamed him Benjamin, which means 'son of the blessing'. This name was often given to the youngest child in the family. He watched over him as he grew. He was afraid that he would lose him too. Reluctantly he agreed to let him travel with his stepbrothers to visit his older brother Joseph, who worked in Egypt. His brothers, knowing their father's concern for his youngest child, looked after him well, and brought him safely home.

Although Jacob continued to worry about Benjamin he grew into a great man and a leader of his people.

Benjamin was the youngest in a large family. What problems do you think he encountered? How do you think he dealt with them?

Benji, Benjie, Bennie, Benny, Ben.

BERNADETTE

16 APRIL

Bernadette Soubirous was born in Lourdes in France in 1844. Her parents were very poor, and Bernadette was quite small and often ill.

One day, when Bernadette was about fourteen years old, she was collecting wood in the forest. Suddenly, she heard the sound of the wind in the bushes, and there, in front of her, in a cloud of gold, she saw a beautiful lady. She stood there looking at her, and in a few moments the lady was gone. Bernadette told no one about what she had seen, but returned to the place again and again, hoping to see the lady once more.

When the lady appeared the second time, she told Bernadette she was Mary, the Mother of Jesus. Later, she told her to drink water from the nearby spring. But Bernadette could not find the spring. She scraped the dry warm earth with her bare hands, and gradually, clear spring water appeared.

Bernadette could not wait to tell everyone what she had seen, but no one believed her. A blind man from the village overheard what she had said, and went with her to the spring. He bathed his eyes, and after a short while, to his amazement, he could see. At last people believed what Bernadette had said. This was the first of many miracles.

Bernadette was always a very prayerful person, and eventually left the village to enter a convent. She remained there until her death on 16th April 1879.

Many people heard about what had happened to Bernadette at Lourdes, and soon the sick and the lame, made the journey to the spring, hoping for a miracle. Today, it is a place of pilgrimage. People travel from all over the world to visit the shrine of Our Lady of Lourdes.

Bernadette chose a life of quiet prayer. Do you find it easy to pray and talk to God about your life?

Berendina, Bern, Berna, Bernadete, Bernarda, Bernarde, Bernardina, Bernie, Nadette, Bernardine

33

CONRAD

21 APRIL

Some people are remembered for the their greatness, their wonderful deeds or their actions in time of trouble. Others like Conrad, are remembered because they were gentle, and kind, but most of all dependable. Conrad was originally called John. He worked on his family farm looking after the fields, meadows and animals in a place called Parzham.

He was a very prayerful person, and in his spare time he loved to visit nearby churches and feel he was close to God. Although he was happy in his work, he knew in his heart that eventually he would like to enter a monastery. For many years he didn't tell his family about his intentions. Finally, at the age of thirty-one he summoned up his courage, and told them he was going to enter the Capuchin monastery as a lay-brother.

It was the custom in those days when joining a religious order, to choose a new name, and John chose the name Conrad. On entering the order he was given the job of welcoming people who came to the door of the monastery. This might seem an insignificant job, but he felt that service to others was service to God. From early morning until late evening, Conrad was there at the door of the monastery. He worked around the clock, welcoming people. They came in their thousands, pilgrims, beggars, children, travellers. Nobody was turned away, no one was disappointed, and Conrad had a smile of welcome for everyone.

His kindness became legendary. People came just to meet this wonderful man. Although he was often tired and exhausted he was always kind and gentle. When people asked him where he got his energy from, he would simply reply, "From prayer."

For forty-one years, Conrad was there at the monastery gate. Finally, he became crippled, and could no longer walk. On the morning of April 18th 1894 he served Mass for the last time. Three days later, while the children to whom he had taught the Rosary, recited it outside his window, Conrad died. The monastery church, where he prayed, is still a place of pilgrimage. People come to honour the memory of the kind and dependable Conrad

> Conrad became a saint by seeing God in everyone he met. How can you see God's goodness in people who come into your life?

Connie, Conny, Conradus, Conroy, Cort, Curt, Konrad, Kort, Kurt

Adalbert

23 APRIL

The story of Adalbert is about a man who always did his best, but no matter how hard he tried, there were those who tormented and rejected him.

Adalbert was born in the year 956 AD. When he was twenty-seven years old he became the Bishop of Prague. He was a deeply spiritual man, and was pleased to have his own diocese. He worked hard, caring for his people, and proclaiming the Christian faith. However, not everyone accepted him or his belief in Christ. He was often tormented and insulted. Finally, his enemies forced him to leave the city. Adalbert was heartbroken. He retreated to a monastery, where he spent his time in prayer.

Several years later, the pope insisted that Adalbert should go back to Prague. Adalbert established a large monastery, and soon Christianity flourished, not only in Prague, but also across Eastern Europe. But there were still those who were opposed to his Christian beliefs, and wanted to destroy him totally. They plotted against him. They killed his brothers and sisters, and once more he was forcefully expelled from Prague. With great sadness he left his beloved city.

He spent his time travelling from one place to another, and finally arrived in the country we now call Poland. He brought the good news of the Gospel to the people. Many listened to him and converted to Christianity, but there were still those who hated the Christians. Tragically, his enemies finally succeeded in destroying him. In the year 997 AD Adalbert was put to death.

> Adalbert kept going through persecution and never gave up. Do you find it difficult to keep doing your best?

Abel, Adalberto, Albert, Aldebert, Bert, Ethelbert

GEORGE

23 APRIL

George is known as someone who was immensely brave. He was a Christian and a soldier in the Roman Empire. His courage was admired and respected by all who knew him.

Legend has it, that a terrifying dragon threatened the city. Every day the dragon demanded a sacrifice of one animal and one human being. If he did not get his way, he threatened to destroy the city. As the dragon took more and more humans and animals, the people became desperate. There was nothing they could do. One by one people in the city were sacrificed. At last it was the turn of a beautiful princess. Her father the king was overcome with grief. He loved his daughter dearly and didn't want to lose her. George decided he would fight the dragon and free the city from this monster. Together with the princess he went to meet the dragon.

Showing no fear George bravely stood before him. The dragon approached, hissing and panting, and with fire pouring from his mouth. George made the sign of the cross, and jumped on his horse. He struck the dragon with his lance. It let out a mighty roar and collapsed onto the ground. With the help of the princess, he bound the dragon with rope and dragged him into the city. There, George killed him with a single blow.

The city was free, and the people were safe. The king was overjoyed and rewarded George with bags of gold. George, not wanting any reward, immediately distributed the gold to the poor. Many years later, under the rule of the new Roman Emperor, Christians were persecuted. George, like many others was captured and killed for his belief in Christ. This brave soldier is now revered as the Patron Saint of England.

The story of George and the dragon is still told today. Although many believe that it was merely a legend; the dragon represents all that is evil, and the princess represents God's holy truth. George, in his bravery, had triumphed over evil.

George was very brave facing the dragon. How do you cope with things that frighten you?

Egor, Georges, Georgie, Georgio, Georgius, Giorgio, Goran, Jerzy, Jorge, Jorgen, Jork, Jürgen, Yuri, York

Mark

25 APRIL

Mark wrote one of the four Gospels, and his symbol is that of a winged lion. He lived with his parents in Jerusalem. It was in their house, that Jesus often met with his disciples and friends. It gave them the opportunity to relax, and discuss the happenings of the day.

After the death of Jesus on the cross, Mark went with the apostle Paul on a trip to Asia Minor. He learned much from Paul who was a wonderful missionary, converting many to Christianity. In contrast to the spirited Paul, Mark was a rather quiet man, and wanted to tell people the good news about Jesus in his own way. This caused them to argue and eventually they separated.

Mark decided to look for Peter. He had always respected Peter, and heard that he was now in Rome. He had been like a father to Mark and Peter used to refer to him as 'my son'. Mark was overjoyed when he eventually found him, and the two men talked and talked for hours. Peter began telling Mark about his time with Jesus and Mark listened intently. Mark started to write down everything Peter said. This was to become the Gospel of Saint Mark, recorded in the New Testament.

When Peter died, Mark moved to Egypt as a missionary, and was a great success. His popularity annoyed those who had rejected Christianity. One day, as he knelt praying at an altar, they captured him. They tied a rope around him, and dragged him down a very long road. Finally they stopped. Mark, who had seen and heard so much, and written so eloquently about Jesus, was dead.

> Mark had a gift for working quietly and telling stories. He used these gifts to write the Gospel. How can you use the gifts you have been given?

Marc, Marco, Marcus, Marek, Marko, Marks, Marx, Merkel, Marcel, Marque, Marcellino, Marcello, Marcellus, Marius

37

29 APRIL

CATHERINE OF SIENNA

Catherine was born the daughter of a wool dyer, in Sienna in Italy in 1347. From a very early age Catherine decided she would not marry, but would devote herself to Jesus. Her family laughed at her. They told her she was only a child, when she grew up she would change her mind and want to be with someone who would care for her.

Some years later, her father Giovanni decided it was time for her to marry. She was still very young, but her parents had already chosen a bridegroom for her. Catherine was upset by their actions, and reminded them that she had vowed never to marry. They didn't take her seriously, and insisted on introducing her to her husband-to-be. But Catherine was defiant, and in front of all three of them, stated that she would never marry anyone. Catherine came from a large family. She had twenty-four brothers and sisters. When they heard of Catherine's refusal, they teased and mocked her. She was also humiliated in front of other members of the family, but she continued in her resolve to devote her life to Jesus.

Several months later, Catherine contracted smallpox, which left her face disfigured by scars. She became reclusive, not wanting to see anyone.

During this time, she experienced wonderful visions, in which Jesus spoke to her. He told her not to give up hope, and reminded her of her vow to dedicate her life to him.

Her parents, seeing that she was determined, relented, and allowed her to enter a convent in Sienna. There she spent long days and nights caring for the sick, always ready to help those in need. The people of Sienna recognised Catherine's devotion, and affectionately called her 'Mama', because of her caring and selfless attitude towards them. If someone was in need, Catherine was there. She was happy in her work. She knew in her heart that in helping others, she was serving Jesus.

> Catherine helped those who came to her with problems.
> How can you help other people to deal with their problems?

Catalina, Caterina, Cathrin, Ina, Ine, Karen, Karin, Kat, Katalin, Kate, Katharine, Kathleen, Kati, Katie, Katina, Katrin, Katy, Kerrin, Kitty,

38

She was an exceptionally intelligent person, who could read, but was unable to write. Nevertheless, people came from far and wide to speak to her. Kings and princes came to ask her advice. Even the pope consulted Catherine if he was unable to find the solution to a particular problem. However, there was always someone ready to criticise. Catherine saw a man shivering from cold, and she gently placed her own coat around his shoulders. This annoyed another man who was standing nearby. He thought she should keep herself warm, and not worry about the other man. Catherine quickly replied that she would rather be without a coat than without love.

As time passed Catherine continued to serve the sick and abandoned. She hardly ate or slept. Finally, completely exhausted, she collapsed, and on 29th April 1380, at the age of just thirty-three years, she died. She had spent her life just as she planned, caring for the needs of others, and thereby serving God. Catherine is one of the Patrons of Europe.

3 MAY — PHILIP AND JAMES

From the first moment that Philip saw Jesus, he was full of admiration for him. He had seen the crowds following Jesus, and sensed there was something special about this man. Many in the crowd called Jesus the Messiah, and the more Philip heard him speak, the more he knew he wanted to become one of his followers. When Jesus eventually asked Philip to join him as an apostle, he considered it a great honour and accepted immediately.

Every day, Philip, together with the other apostles, travelled with Jesus as he preached the good news of God. He watched in wonder as Jesus healed the sick, answered their questions and comforted them.

Once, a huge crowd of about five thousand people gathered to listen to Jesus, and it was getting late. Jesus, seeing that the people were hungry, told his apostles to give them food. But the apostles had little money, certainly not enough to feed so many. A young boy had two small fish and five loaves, which he generously gave to Jesus. Jesus blessed them, and told the apostles to distribute them amongst the people. Philip did not understand. How could so little food feed so many people? He knew he must trust Jesus, and do as he asked. To the amazement of all the apostles there was enough food for everyone.

In the time he spent with Jesus there were many other occasions when Philip put his trust in him. He knew he was the Lord.

James, like Phillip, was also an apostle. After the death of Jesus, he became the Bishop of Jerusalem. He was a good and honest man, which earned him the title 'James the Just'. St Paul even called him a pillar of the Church. The Christians had enemies at this time. Many did not believe in Christ. One day they plotted against James and killed him. James died defending his faith in Christ. In some paintings, James is seen to be holding a book or a club.

Philip and James trusted in Jesus. How can you become trustworthy?

Felipe, Filip, Filippo Phil, Philipp, Philippe, Phillip, Philo

Diego, Giacomo, Hamish, Iacopo, Jack, Jacki, Jacob, Jacopo, Jacques, Jago, Jaime, Jakob, Jameson, Jamie, Jan, Ja, Jim, Jimbo, Jimi, Jimmie, Jimmy, Santiago, Seamus, Shamus, Sheamus

ALEXANDER

3 MAY

Alexander was the fifth pope after Peter, and lived about the year 100 AD. Although the stories told about him are thought to be merely legends, many believe there is always a grain of truth in them.

Alexander was pope at a time of great difficulty for the Church. Many objected to the spread of the Christian faith, and Christians were persecuted and even killed for their beliefs. One day, Alexander was captured and thrown into prison, together with an important man called Hermes. To make sure Alexander did not baptise Hermes, they were put into chains in separate cells and a guard, called Quirinius, supervised them.

One night Quirinius looked into the cell of Hermes. He saw Alexander standing there without chains, and at his side there stood an angel. He quickly ran to Alexander's cell to see how he had escaped. When he arrived, he saw that Alexander was fast asleep. The experience disturbed Quirinius, and when Alexander asked if he would like to be baptised, he agreed.

First, he made it a condition that Alexander would cure his daughter Balbina, who had been very ill. Alexander asked him to bring him the chains, worn by Peter the apostle. Peter had escaped from the chains, when he was imprisoned in Rome. Quirinius brought his daughter Balbina and the chains to Alexander. As she kissed the chains, she was miraculously cured. Later both she and her father were baptised.

The emperor heard of this and was very angry. He ordered the decapitation of Alexander, Quirinius, Balbina and Hermes.

When the news of their deaths, and the miracle which had taken place, reached the people, they wanted to know more about Jesus and many asked to be baptised.

Alexander found the strength to keep going when so many people were against him? How do you find that inner strength when it is needed?

Alastair, Alec, Alejandro, Alek, Alesandro, Alessandro, Alessio, Alex, Alexandre, Alexei, Alexis, Alexius, Alik, Sandie, Sandy

FLORIAN

4 MAY

Florian is the patron saint of fire-fighters. He was born in the third century in a little town near Vienna, which at that time, was ruled by the Romans. One day, Florian was walking past a house and saw it was on fire. There was panic. Many people were emptying buckets of water on the flames, but the fire still burned. Florian calmly took a jug of water and poured it onto the flames. Suddenly, the fire went out. The people were amazed. They couldn't understand how their efforts had failed and yet this young boy, with just a jug of water, had achieved such a miracle.

When Florian grew up, he worked hard and eventually secured a good position with the Roman government. Times became difficult however, when the Romans started to persecute the Christians. His employers did not know he was a Christian, but Florian knew that many of his friends were in danger. Some had even been arrested. Florian could have escaped, but he wanted to support his friends. He didn't want to let them down.

He went directly to the governor, a man called Aquilinus. He stood bravely in front of him and told him he was a Christian. He was greatly respected by Aquilinus, who offered to help him escape. Florian rejected his offer and said that he was ready to die for his belief in Jesus. Aquilinus had no alternative, and Florian was condemned to death.

A heavy stone was put around his neck, and he was thrown into the river, where he drowned. His body was soon washed up on the shore. Immediately, an eagle swooped down and guarded the body from scavengers, until a woman, passing by, placed the body on a cart. She took him away, and gave him a Christian burial.

Florian had a gift for being calm when under pressure. How do you cope when things go wrong?

Flo, Flori, Florianus, Florin, Florinus, Floris

SOPHIE

15 MAY

For many centuries, farmers in Germany have waited until after 'Cold Sophie', the feast of St Sophie, before they planted sensitive seedlings. So often, there have been sudden frosts at this time of year, and their seeds have been destroyed. Four saints, whose feast-days occur during May, Pancratius, Servatius, Boniface and Sophie, are known as the 'Ice Saints'. There is no connection between the lives of these saints and the weather, but their feast-days have become reminders of sudden changes in weather conditions. Farmers pray to these saints for blessings on their fields and crops.

Little is known about the life of Sophie. It is thought that she lived, with her husband and three daughters, in the part of Northern Italy where Milan is today. Her daughters were called Fides, Spes and Caritas meaning Faith, Hope and Charity. Just after Sophie and her family had been baptised as Christians, her husband died. At this tragic time, Sophie found great comfort and strength from her Christian beliefs. She therefore decided to move with her daughters to Rome, to be at the heart of Christianity.

Shortly afterwards, a terrible persecution of the Christians under the Emperor Diocletian, took place. Sophie and her three daughters were arrested and tortured for their faith. They were thrown into prison and died as martyrs. The news of the bravery of Sophie became the talk of Rome. People took her to their hearts and she became known as Sophie of Rome.

? The name Sophie means 'wise person'. Who do you know who is a wise and holy person?

Fey, Fia, Fieke, Sadhbh, Soffia, Sofia, Sofie, Sonja, Sonya, Sophia, Sophronia, Sophy, Zofia

43

JOHN NEPOMUCENE

In some pictures John Nepomucene is portrayed with a halo of five silver stars. These stars are the symbols of the five letters of the Latin word TACUI, which means, 'I was silent'. John Nepomucene refused to break the seal of confession, and his bravery is a reminder to us of how important it is to be able to be trusted with secrets.

John was born in the country, which is now the Czech Republic. When he had finished his studies he became a priest. At that time the king who ruled the country ignored all the laws, and treated his people badly. They were harshly punished for the slightest offence. The queen also suffered at the hands of her violent husband. She had great respect for the priest John Nepomucene, and went to him for confession.

Later, her husband wanted to find out what his wife, the queen, had said in confession. He suspected that she had told the priest how badly he was treating her. He questioned John, but was told quite clearly, that a priest can never tell anyone what he has heard in confession. The king went away in great anger.

Later, to John's surprise, the king invited him to a meal at the palace. During the meal, he made a great fuss of him, and again asked John to tell him what the queen had said in confession. John knew that if he refused the king this time he would be punished. Courageously, he once again refused the information. The king shook with anger, and immediately declared he would kill him.

On 16th May 1393, John was bound, hands and feet. A stone was tied to his neck and he was pushed off a bridge into a river, where he drowned. It is said that, after his death, his body was often seen surrounded by light. In many countries in Europe there is still a tradition today of placing a statue of John Nepomucene on bridges. This serves as a reminder of a good man who died defending his beliefs.

John did not break the seal of confession. Can you keep promises and secrets when it is right to do so?

Eoin, Evan, Gianni, Giovanni, Hans, Hanke, Hanko, Hannemann, Hannes, Hans, Iaian, Ian, Ivan, Iven, Iwan, Jack, Jan, Jannis, Jean, Johann, Juan, Nino, Seain, Sean, Shane, Shawn, Zane

18 MAY

FELIX

The word 'Felix' means 'happy'. Saints were happy people, and there are many saints in the history of the Church who bear the name Felix. On 18th May we commemorate Felix of Cantalice who was very popular with children.

Felix was born in the village of Cantalice in Umbria in Italy in the year 1515. His parents were peasants and, from a very early age, he was destined to be a shepherd. He remained on the farm for over twenty years, first as a shepherd-boy and afterwards as a farm labourer. Felix was never happier than when he was saying his prayers. He even carved a crucifix for himself in the trunk of a big tree, beside the meadow where he tended the sheep.

When Felix was 30 years old, he said good-bye to his parents and brothers and sisters, and went off to join a monastery in Rome. For over forty years he devoted his time to the service of his community. The monks had no source of income, and Felix went from house to house begging for food and money for the monastery. Whenever someone gave him an offering he would say,
"Give thanks to God."
People heard him say this so often, they renamed this little man, in a brown monk's habit, 'Brother Deogratias'. This is Latin for 'Give thanks to God'. It is said, that during the famine of 1580, the directors of the city's charities asked his superiors to give Felix permission to collect money to provide food for the hungry. This he did, with great success.

Felix was well liked with the local children. As they gathered around him, he would form them into a circle, and teach them little songs he had composed. Their singing became very popular with the people. Often, when he was on his rounds begging for food, Felix would be invited into their houses to sing with the children. Eventually, the songs became so well known that the whole town joined in with the singing.

Felix is often represented in paintings, holding the Child Jesus. There is a legend that the Blessed Virgin Mary appeared to him and placed the Divine Child in his arms. This is probably why he was chosen as the patron saint of mothers. Felix of Cantalice died on the 18th May 1587.

Felix kept close to God by being cheerful and thankful. Do you find it easy to say 'thank-you' and stay cheerful?

Felice, Felicius, Felizian, Felizianus, Felizius

RITA

22 MAY

From a very early age Rita had always wanted to be a nun. As she grew up, she continued to tell everyone this was her dearest wish. Her parents recognised her determination, but worried that if she entered a convent, they might never see her again. They decided that, to prevent Rita from dedicating her life solely to God, they would choose a husband for her. Rita was a dutiful daughter, and to please her parents, she decided she would marry the man they had chosen, and become a good and faithful wife to her husband.

In time she gave birth to two fine sons, who brought her much joy. However, the marriage was not happy. Her husband was a violent man who often beat her. One day her husband was involved in a fight and was killed. Her two sons swore revenge on whoever had done the terrible deed; they wanted to kill the murderer. This terrified Rita, and she prayed to God. She would rather see her sons die, than to commit a murder. Shortly afterwards, both her sons died from natural causes.

Rita was heartbroken, she loved her sons so much and now they were gone. After many months of sorrow, she decided it was time to begin again and to spend the rest of her life as she had always desired. She entered a little convent in Cascia, and spent the next forty years in the service of God.

In 1447 when Rita was close to death, she was asked if there was anything she wanted. "I would like a rose from the garden," she answered quietly.

It was now deep winter, and nothing was growing in the convent garden, but there, on the leafless rosebush, was a beautiful fresh rose. Rita was given the rose and wept with joy. She closed her eyes and died peacefully.

Today, roses are always used as a remembrance of St Rita. Every year, on 22nd May, in many countries, rose petals are blessed and distributed amongst the sick. Throughout her life Rita had never given up hope, and is known as the patron saint of hopeless cases.

> Rita's love of God kept her going through her difficult and tragic life. What keeps you going when you encounter difficulties?

Margareta, Margarete, Margherita

47

Julia

Little is known about Julia. It is thought that she was a young girl who came from Carthage in North Africa. She believed in Jesus Christ and was very devout. She would often visit the church, to say her prayers and to be close to God.

When hostile soldiers conquered her city, the invaders captured the young Christian girls and women. They took them away on sailing ships to other countries, to work as slaves. A man called Eusebius captured Julia, and forced her to sail away with him.

Julia was terrified. She searched the ship for somewhere to hide, somewhere no one would find her. During this time she never lost her belief in Jesus Christ. Every day she prayed to him to give her strength to bear this terrible ordeal.

The ship headed towards the island of Corsica in the Mediterranean, where it stopped to take on more provisions. There, Julia was captured once more, this time by the inhabitants of the island. A few days later she was killed. They had tied her to a wooden cross, and left her without food or water until she was dead.

Her body remained on the island until kindly monks later brought it to safety. It is thought that Julia died in the year 439 AD. Today the town of Brescia in Northern Italy has a church dedicated to Julia, the young girl who suffered and died many years ago for her belief in Christ.

Julia kept close to God even when she felt frightened and alone. How can you stay close to God when you think friends have deserted you?

Gill, Gillian, Giulia, Giuliana, Giulietta, Iliane, Jill, Jula, Jula, Julchen, Jule, Jules, Juliana, Juliane, Julie, Julienne, Juliet, Juliette, Julita, Lia, Liane, Lilli

Philip Neri

26 MAY

Philip Neri was highly respected by the people of Rome. It has been said he was one of the nicest saints because he had such a wonderful personality. He was always cheerful and had a smile for everyone.

Philip was a brilliant man. He had spent many long hours studying, poring over books, and absorbing knowledge about a great many things. But Philip wanted more. He wanted to help people, and not spend his life surrounded by books. He decided to become a priest and was ordained in 1551.

His interest in people was obvious from the start. They flocked to his services, and his church was so full, people had to stand outside. His love of God and love of his people endeared him to everyone. Children also loved 'Pippo Buono', the Good Philip, as they called him. Soon his congregation was so large he had to hire a hall so that everyone could hear him.

They had never experienced anything like it. Jugglers, singers and musicians performed, and there in the middle was Philip telling people about Jesus.

He showed them how enjoyable he thought religion should be, and the people were grateful. He also knew that if his work was to continue after his death, he had to plan ahead. He established a religious community called the Oratorians, who were to continue his work with love and dedication. Philip Neri died in 1595 just before his 80th birthday, but the people of Rome never forgot him.

Philip reminds us that religion does not have to be dull. How do you think religion could be more enjoyable?

Felipe, Filip, Filippo Phil, Philipp, Philippe, Phillip, Philo

30 MAY

JOAN OF ARC

The life of Joan of Arc has been recorded in both art and literature. It still captures the imagination, centuries after her death. She was born into a poor farming family in Domremy in France in 1412. For many years the country was in turmoil. A terrible war with England had broken out and English soldiers were fighting on French soil. They conquered large parts of France, including Paris.

When Joan was about twelve years old, she heard a voice saying,
"Help your king and rescue France."
Joan was scared to tell anyone. She knew they would not take any notice of her, they would think she had made it up. She couldn't help France. She had never received a formal education, and could not even read or write, people wouldn't believe her.

She continued to hear the voice. For four years she heard it again and again. When the soldiers eventually reached the city of Arc, she was desperate. The voice now said,
"Hurry Joan, free the city of Arc."

She knew she had to tell someone and confided in her uncle. Nervously she started to tell him about the voice, she thought he would think she was mad.

But the uncle was a wise man, who was desperate to do something to help his country, and he believed Joan. He immediately took Joan to the leader of the French army. The man just laughed at her and told her uncle to take her home and keep her in order.

However, when Joan began telling the citizens details about the battles so far, they demanded action. They pleaded with the army to let Joan speak to the king, Charles VII. He was afraid the people would revolt if he didn't do something, and so he reluctantly agreed to see her. By this time Joan was no longer afraid, she knew what she had to do.

She marched courageously to her meeting with the king, and told him things that only he could have known. The king soon realised that this young girl was the only one who could help him, and save the whole of France. He promptly handed the leadership of the army over to Joan.

Joan heard God speaking in her heart. Have you ever felt that God has spoken in your heart?

Anusia, Gianna, Giovanna, Hanja, Hanka, Hanna, Hannah, Hanne, Hannerl, Hanni, Ivana, Ivanna, Jana, Jane, Janet, Janina, Janine, Janka, Janna, Janne, Janula, Jeanne, Jeannette, Jehanna, Jehanne, Jenny , Joanne, Johann,

The morale of the French army was low. They couldn't see any way of freeing the city of Arc. Suddenly, before them came a young girl, riding a horse. They couldn't believe their eyes. She was dressed in full armour, and was ready to lead them into battle. Through her prayers and determination, she encouraged the men to take on the English army once more. Soon they won battle after battle, and the city of Arc was free. The whole city cheered Joan. She stood beside the king holding a victory banner and shouting, "Now, God's will has been done."

Joan was eager to free Paris, but her courage and success had made her many enemies. They managed to convince the king that the charges against her were true, and the weak king decided Joan would no longer lead his army into battle. Joan was captured and handed over to the English soldiers. Following much suffering and humiliation, she was finally burnt at the stake in the city of Rouen in May 1431. She was just nineteen years old.

BONIFACE

5 JUNE

Winfrid was a devout Benedictine monk, whose dream was to share God's message with others. He wanted to be a missionary, but his opportunity to take Christianity to other lands did not happen until he was forty-three years old. He travelled to Germany, but was not well received by local people and he was forced to return to his native England.

Later, with permission from Pope Gregory II, he returned to Germany once more. By now his name had been changed to Boniface, which means 'Doer of Good', and he was even more determined. He travelled across Germany preaching and baptising wherever he went. In the year 723 AD Boniface visited a place where the people worshiped an oak tree as their god. He was very angry at what he saw. He took a large axe, prayed to God and with a mighty blow chopped down the tree. As the gigantic oak hit the ground, it spilt into four equal parts. The people were amazed at the miracle that had taken place before their eyes. They now believed that the God, to whom Boniface prayed, was mightier than the giant oak. They pleaded with Boniface to tell them more about God, and baptise them. They wanted to become Christians. Inspired by what they heard, they helped Boniface to build a little church out of the wood from the oak tree.

In time, Boniface and his followers converted thousands to Christianity. He established dioceses, monasteries and churches, and Christianity in Germany flourished. He became the Bishop of Mainz. In the year 754 AD, when he was eighty years old, he decided to return to the place in Germany where he had first tried to start his missionary work. Sadly, he was met with even more aggression than before. Boniface and his fifty-two fellow missionaries were attacked and killed. Although he was born in England, Boniface will always have a special place in the hearts of the German people. It is because of him Christianity still flourishes in Germany today.

Boniface means 'doing good'. What good have you done for others recently?

Bonifacio, Bonifatios, Bonifaz, Bonifazio, Bonifazius, Bonnie, Bonny, Bonus, Faas, Facius

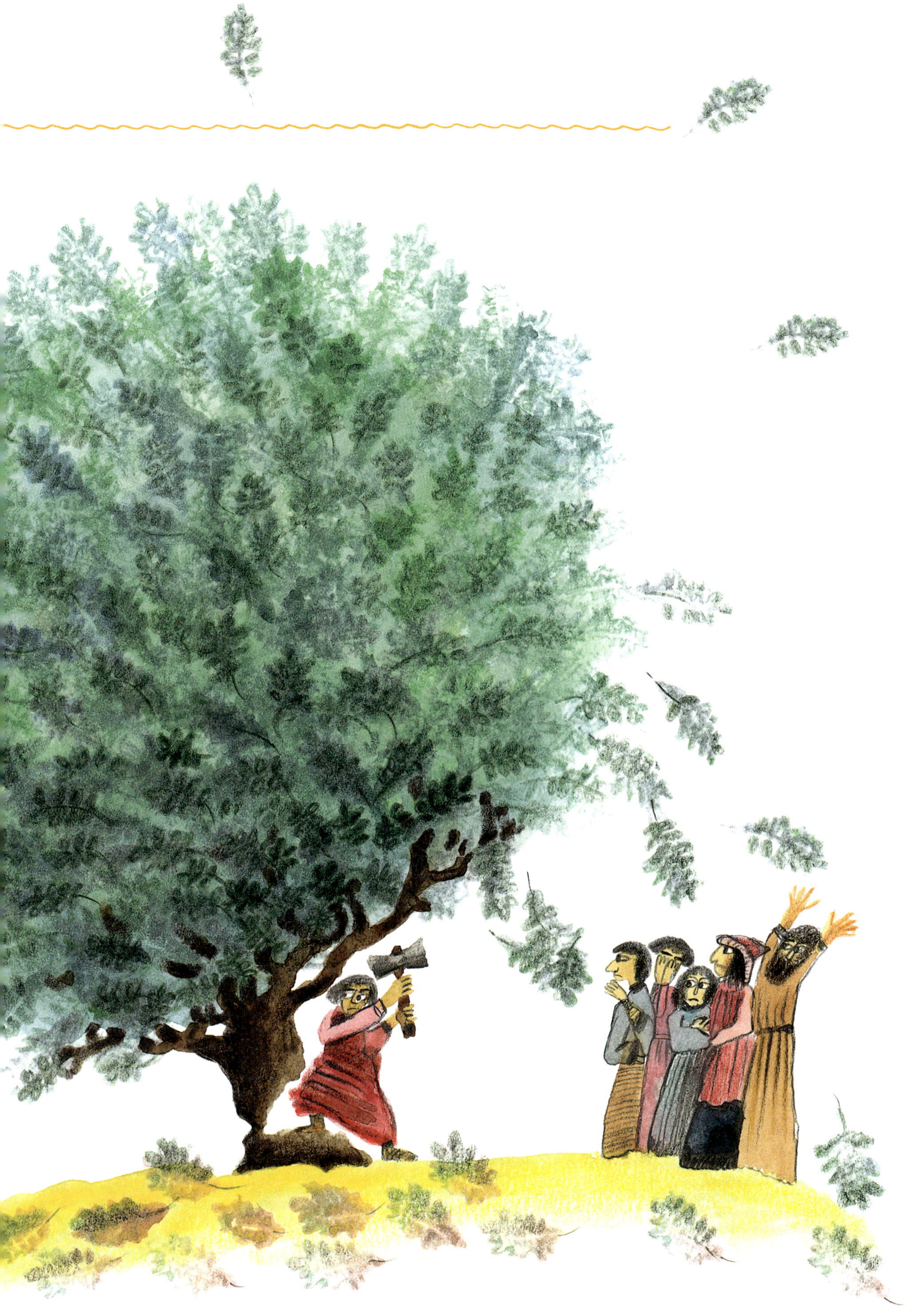

ANTHONY OF PADUA

13 JUNE

Fernandez Bulhoes was born in Portugal in 1190. He became a Franciscan monk and took the name Anthony. He later moved to Italy and there he met the founder of the Franciscan order, Francis of Assisi. When Francis heard Anthony preach he realised he had a wonderful gift. He asked him to visit different cities in Italy preaching and telling people about Jesus Christ. Anthony saw this as an important task and was eager to begin.

Thousands came to listen to his exciting sermons. However, in some cities Anthony was not greeted so enthusiastically. Once, in a place called Rimini, Anthony preached to an empty church. This saddened him and he went to the beach to pray. As he walked along the water's edge he prayed out loud. He asked God to help him at this difficult time in his ministry. He looked at the shimmering sea, and to his amazement the fish had pushed their heads out of the water and were listening intently to his prayers. Anthony decided to continue to preach with only the fish as his congregation. When he had finished he turned around and saw a crowd had gathered. They too were listening to him and praying with him. In preaching to the fish, many more had heard his words and believed.

Anthony continued to travel and to preach to even greater numbers. He worked tirelessly bringing God's message to others. Finally, exhausted by his journeys he returned to the silence of the monastery, and was often seen sitting quietly in the garden praying.

Anthony died in 1231, and is buried in Padua, Italy. Many people have a great devotion to St Anthony and pray to him to find items they have lost or mislaid.

Anthony could make the Gospel come alive in words. How can you make the Gospel come alive in the way you talk and act with family and friends?

Antal, Antoine, Anton, Antonello, Antonin, Antonino, Antoninus, Antonio, Antony, Tone, Toni, Tonino, Tonio, Tony

JOHN THE BAPTIST

24 JUNE

Elizabeth and Zechariah loved each other deeply. Many years after their marriage, an angel appeared to Zechariah and told him they would soon have a son and he would be called John. Zechariah was so surprised he couldn't speak. They had been married for many years and longed for a child. The angel promised him that once the child was born, his speech would return.

Later, Elizabeth had a visit from her cousin Mary. She told her she was going to be the mother of Jesus. When Mary heard that Elizabeth was also with child, the two women hugged each other with joy. When her baby was born, Elizabeth wanted to name him after his father. But Zechariah remembered what the angel had told him and wrote down the name 'John'. From that moment his speech returned.

John grew into a good and honest man. He wanted to devote his life to serving God. He had seen the sinful lives of people around him and went into the desert to pray. He lived on locusts and wild honey and wore a simple cloth. Whilst there, God spoke to him and asked him to prepare the way for Jesus. From that moment John knew what he must do. He left the desert and went back to the city. He spent his time talking to people and telling them about God. He asked them to lead less sinful lives.

News of this great preacher quickly spread. People came from all parts of the country to hear what he had to say. They had been promised a Messiah, and they thought that it was John. But John humbly told them that he was not the one. He was only preparing the way for the one who would save them.

Later, when it was time for Jesus to start his ministry, he was walking beside the River Jordan when he saw John baptising a crowd of people. He stopped and asked John to baptise him too. John recognised him and knelt down before him. He said, "I am not worthy to baptise you. It is you that should be baptising me."

Jesus told him that they should do what God asks of them. John baptised Jesus, and as he was doing so, the clouds opened. A dove appeared and the voice of God was heard, "This is my son. My beloved son."
The people looked at Jesus in awe and wondered if he was the promised Messiah.

John continued to spread God's message, but his popularity came to the notice of King Herod. He felt John was becoming too influential. He had so many people following him and listening to God's word, he thought he might be a threat to his throne. Full of hatred, he had John thrown into prison and then killed. John's life was over, but he had completed the task set for him by God. He had prepared the way for Jesus, the Promised One.

> John was one of the first people to recognise Jesus. How could you recognise the goodness of Jesus in your friends and family?

Eoin, Evan, Gianni, Giovanni, Hans, Hanke, Hanko, Hannemann, Hannes, Hans, Iaian, Ian, Ivan, Iven, Iwan, Jack, Jan, Jannis, Jean, Johann, Juan, Nino, Seain, Sean, Shane, Shawn, Zane

29 JUNE

PETER AND

On 29th June in the year 258 AD, the Roman Emperor Valerian decreed that all Christian burial places in Rome should be destroyed. As soon as this was announced, a group of devout Christians took the remains of Peter and Paul and hid them. This was the start of a great devotion to these two saints, and is said to be the reason why their feast day is celebrated together on 29th June every year. But Peter and Paul were also linked in other ways. Without their hard work and dedication, God's message would never have been spread so successfully throughout the world. Christianity can be compared to a house. Peter put down the foundations. Paul erected the walls and roof, and his missionary work filled the house with people.

Peter was a simple fisherman who was chosen by Jesus as one of his apostles. Jesus recognised the inner strength of Peter, and eventually chose him to be his successor in spreading God's message. Although Peter had all the qualities to be a leader, he also had human weaknesses. When Jesus was in prison, Peter denied knowing him three times because he was afraid that he too would be captured. But Jesus understood this and forgave him. Later he told him,
"You art Peter, and upon this rock I will build my Church."
The name Peter means 'rock' or 'strength'. He also entrusted Peter with the work of looking after the Christian community, which had now been established. He said,
"Feed my lambs, feed my sheep."

Following the ascension of Jesus, Peter began his mission, travelling far and wide, spreading the good news of God to the people. Many years later he arrived in Rome, where Christianity was flourishing. For years he cared for the people and became the first Bishop of Rome, and the first Pope. However, the time came when the Roman Emperor, Nero, decided to persecute Christians. Peter was captured and crucified upside down on a cross. On the site in Rome where this happened, a great basilica was built in his memory, the Basilica of St Peter.

58

Paul

Paul was originally named Saul. As a young man he hated everyone who believed in Jesus. He persecuted many Christians, and through him the deacon Stephen was put to death. One day on the road to Damascus, Saul had a vision. A bright light shone, and he was thrown off his horse. Paul heard the voice of Jesus asking him why he was persecuting him. From that day onwards he was a changed man. He became known as Paul and was filled with a deep love of Christ.

He took it upon himself to make up for the wrong he had done in the past. He was determined to spread God's message to non-believers throughout the world. He started on foot, and then by boat, through Asia Minor, Cyprus, Macedonia and Greece. He travelled thousands of miles and was an inspiring preacher. He filled everyone with such enthusiasm that Christian communities sprung up wherever he preached.

Many years later, he arrived in Rome and was arrested and imprisoned for his faith. He was a learned man, who wrote many letters, some of which were from his prison cell. These letters are still valued by the Church today. Later, Paul was condemned to death and killed with a sword. His remains are buried in the Basilica of Saint Paul in Rome, which is visited by many thousands of pilgrims every year.

> Both Peter and Paul made mistakes and found it hard to admit their weakness. Do you find it easy to admit mistakes and to say you are sorry?

Peder, Pedro, Peer, Peko, Pes, Petar, Pete, Petr, Petros, Petz, Pier, Piero, Pierre, Pierrin, Pierrot, Piet, Pieter, Pietro, Piotre

Pagel, Pale, Pals, Paolino, Paolo, Paulinus, Paulos, Pauw, Pawel

59

3 JULY

THOMAS

Thomas was a fisherman, who became one of the apostles of Jesus. He loved and trusted Jesus and was happy to follow him. He is remembered not only for the time he spent with Jesus, but also for something that happened after Jesus had risen from the dead.

Two of the disciples had been walking along the road to Emmaus, when a stranger joined them. They invited him to eat with them. It wasn't until they saw the way he broke bread with them, that they realised it was Jesus. When they returned to Jerusalem, they told the others what had happened. Suddenly, to their surprise, Jesus appeared before them once more. Thomas was not present at the time. When the others excitedly told him they had seen the risen Christ, he didn't believe them. He wanted proof.

"Unless I can see his wounds, I won't believe he has been here."

A few days later Jesus appeared to them again. He looked sadly at Thomas,

"Look at my wounds. Touch the scars. Now do you believe it is me?"

Thomas knelt down before him, and quietly said,

"My Lord and my God."

Jesus said,

"You believe because you can see me. Happy are those who believe but have not seen me."

Thomas was sorry he had not believed.

Even to-day, thousands of years later, he is remembered as 'Doubting Thomas'.

After the coming of the Holy Spirit, Thomas, together with the rest of the followers of Jesus, started their work, spreading Christ's message. Later, Thomas travelled to other countries. Finally, in the year 52 AD, he arrived in India. His mission work continued, and thousands were converted to Christianity. He stayed in India many years, but was eventually tortured and killed by his enemies in the year 70 AD. The people of India have a special devotion to St Thomas and every year they celebrate the day he first arrived in their land. He was so loved by the people, they erected a church in Madras on the spot where he died.

Thomas found it hard to believe but trusted in Jesus. Do you find it hard to believe sometimes?

Masetto, Maso, Tamás, Tamme, Tammes, Thoma, Thomé, Thommy, Tom, Toma, Tomas, Tomaso, Tomes, Tomis, Tommaso, Tommy, Tomy

Ulric

4 JULY

Pictures of Ulric show him riding a horse or with a plate of fish. Two different animals, and two very different stories.

Ulric was born the son of a count in Augsburg, Germany in the year 890 AD. He decided very early in his life, that he wanted to become a priest. After he was ordained he was soon chosen to be a bishop. He was highly respected, and was appointed to positions of responsibility in the Church. He became famous as a result of an event, which occurred in the year 955 AD. Hungarian soldiers were preparing to attack the city of Augsburg. The emperor's army, which was supposed to be defending the city, had no leader and were just waiting in the city for the enemy to attack. Bishop Ulric realised that the army needed a leader, so he took command. He asked the population to pray in silence as he rode out on a horse, leading the army against the enemy. The army, led by Ulric, put up a brave fight until the Emperor arrived with his army and defeated the enemy.

Then there is the story of the fish. A good friend of Ulric's came to visit him late one Thursday evening. Ulric welcomed him and put a meal before him. They sat talking late into the night, totally forgetful of the time. The visitor suddenly realised that it was time to go; it was already time for breakfast. The visitor was in a hurry and as he prepared to leave, Ulric invited him to eat some of the food left over from the previous day's supper. The remains of some meat still lay on the plate. Ulric had completely forgotten that it was already Friday, and in those days Christians did not eat meat on Friday.

Suddenly, a messenger from the duke arrived to deliver a letter to Ulric. Naturally Ulric invited the messenger to have a bite to eat. The messenger immediately rode off to the duke, to tell him that the bishop was a hypocrite, because he ate meat on Friday. He had carefully brought a piece of the meat with him as proof. When he took the meat out of the bag to show the duke, it had changed into a fish. The messenger was highly embarrassed, and Ulric's good name was preserved. Bishop Ulric died in Augsburg in the year 973 AD.

Ulric had the qualities to become a leader. What qualities do you think you need to lead others?

Ohlsen, Ole, Olsen, Udalrich, Udelrico, Udo, Ueli, Uhl, Ule, Uli, Ulli, Ullrich, Ullus Ulrico, Ulrik

BENEDICT

11 JULY

Although Benedict lived over 15 hundred years ago, he helped to shape European culture. He is revered as a Patron of Europe. He and his twin sister Scholastica were born in Umbria in Italy in the year 480 AD. After his parents had given him an excellent education he moved to Rome to study to be a lawyer. But Benedict did not like what he saw in Rome. People had little respect for each other or for themselves. Many no longer believed in Christ. Benedict decided to give up his studies and escape to the mountains where he could be alone with his thoughts and prayers.

Some time later, monks from a nearby abbey heard about this 'strange' man who had chosen to leave city life behind him. They visited him and were surprised to find a devout, well-educated man living in a cave. They recognised that this was just the man they needed. They invited him to join them as leader of their community. Benedict rejected their offer at first. He didn't think that community life with monks was what he wanted. He later reconsidered the offer and took up the post as abbot.

Some members of the community objected to Benedict organising them, telling them what they could and could not do. They resented his interference. They insulted him and plotted against him, and one even wanted to kill him. He gave Benedict poisoned bread to eat, but Benedict found out just in time. Reluctantly, he left the abbey and retreated once more to his cave.

These events convinced him that the monks needed to be more organised; they needed rules. Not just spoken rules but a book of rules with clear instructions. They needed guidelines by which they could live. With determination Benedict decided to organise his ideas. He formulated them in what is now known as 'The Rule of Saint Benedict'.

Eventually, he gathered together small groups of men who wanted to devote themselves to God, and were willing to accept the rules. They all wore similar black clothing, making them the same before God and man. As more and more men wanted to join, small religious communities were formed, and they took the name Benedictines. With their own hands they built their monasteries. The most famous of these stands on a mountain between Rome and Naples, the monastery of Monte Cassino.

From it's humble beginnings, in a cave on a lowly mountain, Benedict's ideas on the organisation of monastic life soon became accepted by the rest of the world. In the year 547 AD when Benedict died peacefully, he was buried in Monte Cassino beside his beloved twin sister Scholastica.

> Benedict became holy by remembering God in work, in prayer and in relaxation. When do you find it easiest to remember that God is with you?

Ben, Bene, Benedetto, Benedicht, Bénédict, Benedicto, Benedictus, Benito, Bennet, Benny, Benno, Bénoît

13 JULY

HENRY AND CUNEGUNDES

Henry was born of noble birth in Bavaria in the year 973 AD. When he was just 22 years old he became a duke, and seven years later a German king. His role as king was a heavy burden because his predecessor had not ruled wisely. There was a great deal of crime and unrest in the country and people had lost their faith in God. Henry was a popular king. He had a great love for his people, and set about the task of ruling the country with honesty and devotion to God.

He organised new dioceses and appointed over forty new bishops. He founded new convents and abbeys, and, by his example, brought thousands back to God. His wife Cunegundes supported him in his work and their devotion to each other was clear for everyone to see. However, some were jealous of their happiness and spread malicious gossip about her. They accused her of being unfaithful. When Henry heard these accusations about his wife, he was heartbroken. She had always been his loyal and faithful wife. To prove her innocence she walked with bare feet on burning coals. To the amazement of her enemies, she remained completely unharmed by the glowing embers.

On 14th February 1014, Henry and Cunegundes were crowned Emperor and Empress of Germany. Henry became known as 'The Sacred Emperor'. Ten years later in 1024 he died, followed nine years later by Cunegundes. Death had reunited this loving and devoted couple.

> Henry was heartbroken when he heard people gossiping about his wife. How can you stop people saying bad things about others?

Arrigo, Endrik, Enrico, Enrique, Enzio, Genrich, Harry, Heiko, Heinar, Heiner, Heini, Heinke, Heino, Heinz, Heise, Hendrik, Henke, Henner, Hennes, Henri, Henrik Henryk, Hinrich, Hinz, Jindrich.

Cunégonde, Gundel, Konne, Kuni, Kunihild, Kunna

Margaret

20 JULY

Margaret was born, in the third century, in Antioch, which is now part of Syria. Her father Theodosius sent her to be educated and raised by a nanny. However, he did not know the nanny was a Christian. She taught Margaret to know and love Jesus Christ, and when her father discovered this, he was furious. He didn't believe in Jesus and demanded that Margaret no longer practised her faith. When Margaret refused, he took her to see Olybrius the Roman governor, who hated the Christians.

As soon as Olybrius saw Margaret, he was overwhelmed by her beauty and wanted to marry her. He offered to ignore the accusations against her, in return for her hand in marriage. Margaret refused. She told him she loved only Jesus, and had no wish to marry anyone. Olybrius was angry. He felt insulted by her refusal, and he had her cruelly tortured. Her badly wounded body was thrown into prison. Later, he went to her cell to speak to her. When he arrived, he couldn't believe his eyes. Margaret showed no sign of her injuries. She was as beautiful as ever, without a single mark or wound.

The following night a gigantic dragon appeared before Margaret. It tried to coil itself around her, and at the same time the cell was filled with a bright light. Through the dazzling brightness Margaret saw a dove. Summoning up all her strength, she hit the dragon, and it fell dead on the ground. Olybius witnessed this, and the next day, full of fear, he had her killed.

Before she died she prayed to God for strength. Today, those in need, especially mothers, pray to St Margaret to intercede for them, and to ask for God's help.

Margaret refused to give in to evil and trusted God. Have you the courage to do that in your own world?

Gesche, Gitta, Greta, Gretel, Grit, Gritta, Madge, Mag, Magga, Maggie, Maret, Marga, Margalita, Margarete, Margaretha, Margarethe, Margarita, Margery, Margherita, Margit, Margita, Margone, Margot, Margotine, Margret, Margrit, Marguérite, Marit, Marjorie, Marketta, Meg, Merit, Merita, Meta, Peggy, Reta, Rita

DANIEL

21 JULY

Daniel lived 600 years before the birth of Christ. He was a devout Jew living in Jerusalem. When war broke out, the city fell into the hands of the Babylonian king, Nebuchadnezzar, and Daniel was captured. However, the king soon recognised his worth and ordered him to work in his court. Daniel was reluctant, but knew it was a chance for him to survive. He also knew that if it was what God wanted, he should trust the Lord and obey the king's command.

Daniel settled well into the court and soon gained the king's respect. Later, when disturbing dreams troubled the king, he sent for Daniel and asked for his advice. He watched as Daniel knelt down to pray for God's guidance. He asked God to give him the wisdom to interpret King Nebuchadnezzar's dreams. To the amazement of the king, Daniel was able to explain the meaning of each dream in detail. The king was filled with awe at the interpretations. He acknowledged that the god to whom Daniel prayed must indeed be the one true God.

Many years later a new king came to the throne. Daniel was an old man by now, but still remained close to the sovereign. He had become the king's confidante. Before the king made any important decisions, every issue was discussed with Daniel. This angered other courtiers. They were jealous of Daniel's closeness to the throne and plotted to kill him. They threatened the king with violence if he did not get rid of Daniel. The king had no choice, and reluctantly condemned Daniel to death.

As his enemies stood by, Daniel was thrown into a pit of hungry lions. Loudly they roared and snarled. Daniel looked into their fiery eyes and prayed to God to save him. Suddenly, the roaring stopped, the lions were calm and Daniel was safe. God had protected him from his enemies. They had tried to destroy him and they had failed. Daniel knew, that if he put his trust in him, God would not forsake him.

Because others threatened him, the king treated Daniel badly. How would you make the right choice under pressure?

Dan, Dane, Daniele, Danil, Danilo, Dannel, Danni, Danny, Dano

67

MARY MAGDALENE

22 JULY

Mary Magdalene was an important person in the life of Jesus. She was one of the few women amongst his followers. He had cured her of a terrible illness and she believed in him and trusted him. She knew that he was the Messiah, the one the whole of Israel had waited for. Many people called her a sinner and thought Jesus should not associate with her. But Jesus had forgiven her sins. He asked her enemies to look into their own hearts, to see if they were without sin themselves.

On the day that Jesus died on the cross, Mary Magdalene stood with Mary the mother of Jesus and the apostle John. They heard the yelling of the crowd and the insults of the soldiers. Other followers of Jesus were so afraid, they had gone into hiding, but Mary Magdalene stood there, watching, and comforting his mother. She remained at the foot of the cross, until Jesus had drawn his last breath. She watched as he was laid in the tomb.

Three days later Mary Magdalene, and a few friends, went to visit the place where Jesus was buried. The large stone that had been placed at the entrance was rolled aside and the tomb was empty. Mary Magdalene and her friends were worried. They thought someone had stolen the body. An angel appeared and told them Jesus had risen from the dead. Suddenly, Jesus appeared in front of them. He told them to return to Galilee and tell the apostles what they had seen. Eagerly, Mary ran into the city, and shared with them the good news of the resurrection.

? Mary's friendship with Jesus grew through forgiveness. Do you find it easy to forgive your friends when mistakes are made?

Mae, Maia, Maike, Maire, Maja, Mami, Manon, Marei, Maria, Mareike, Mareile, Marella, Maren, Mariana, Marica, Maricke, Marie, Marieka, Marieke, Mariella, Marietta, Marihuela, Marija, Marijke, Marike, Marilyn, Marinetta, Marinka, Marion, Maris, Mariska, Marita, Maritta, Marja, Marka, Maruscha, Maruska Marya, Mascha, Maschinka, Maura, Maureen, May, Meike, Mia, Mieke, Mieze, Mimi, Minnie, Miriam, Mirjam, Mirl, Mitzi, Mizzi, Ria

Alena, Alina, Leli, Lena, Lene, Lenelle, Leni, Lenka, Lona, Maddalena, Maddy, Madeleine, Madelena, Madelina, Madeline, Mädi, Madina, Madlen, Madlenka, Madlon, Mado, Mady, Magalonne, Magda, Magdalen, Magdalene, Magdali, Magdelina, Magdolna, Magel, Maggy, Malen, Malene, Malin, Malina, Marlene, Maud

69

BRIDGET

23 JULY

At a very young age a marriage was arranged between Bridget and the son of a nobleman. Although she was forced into the marriage, she learned to love her husband and bore him eight children. Bridget was a perfect wife and mother. When she was only forty-one years old her husband died. She was so heartbroken that she entered a convent to be alone with her thoughts and prayers.

At that time there was a great deal of lawlessness in the country. People didn't take responsibility for their actions, and had little respect for each other. One day, as Bridget sat quietly praying, she heard an inner voice.

It was as if God was speaking to her. He asked her to work amongst the people, and help them to be more law-abiding and to lead more responsible and faithful lives.

Bridget knew what she must do. Faced with a new challenge she was eager to begin. She immediately went to Rome to start a new religious order. She worked with the rich and the poor, showing them how to care for each other, and how to lead better lives. This was the start of Bridget's unceasing work for others. Gradually people started to change. They became more responsible and learned to live in harmony with each other. News of her work quickly spread, and she was admired and respected by everyone.

When she died in July 1373, thousands watched and mourned as her body was taken from Rome, back to Sweden. Even today Christians admire St Bridget, as one of the patrons of Europe.

Bridget helped people get on together and live as a community. How could we help people to get on together?

Berit, Berrit, Birgid, Birgida, Brid, Briddy, Bride, Bridie, Briga, Brigga, Brigida, Brigitta, Brigitte, Brit, Britt, Gitta, Gitte

CHRISTOPHER

24 JULY

Christopher was born in the third century in Asia Minor, in the country now called Turkey. He was a large baby and his parents named him Reprobus. He grew big and strong. One day as he looked for suitable work, he met a hermit who had built a house near the river. The two men started talking. The hermit suggested Reprobus should use his strength to carry people across the river. Many people had wanted to cross to the distant shore, but it was very deep in parts. Reprobus was delighted with this suggestion. Very soon he was transporting people backwards and forwards on his broad shoulders.

One day a little child stood in front of him. He asked to be carried to the other side. Reprobus did not hesitate. He gently lifted the child onto his shoulders and started to cross the river. The further he walked, the heavier the child became. It took all of his strength to carry him, and he prayed that he would reach the other side. When he finally got to the shore, he put down the child and collapsed, exhausted. The child looked at him and told him he was Jesus Christ. He also told him that from now on he should be called Christopher, because he had carried Christ.

It is believed that many years later, Christopher was killed by Roman soldiers because of his Christian beliefs. It is also thought that Christ's message to Reprobus was that life's journey was not easy, but with God's help he would succeed. The name Christopher has come to mean 'Christ Bearer', and Christopher has become the patron saint of travellers.

Like Christopher, we all have strengths. How do you use your strengths to help others?

Christoph, Christoffer, Christof, Chris, Kristoffer, Kristof, Christophe, Cristoforo, Christóbal, Christo, Cristo, Krysztof, Chrystal, Kristofer, Christof, KristofKris, Kit, Christophe, Kester, Cristobel.

71

CHRISTINA

24 JULY

Christina's parents were not Christian. They worshipped a pagan god. In the area around Bolsena in Italy where they lived, more and more people were converting to Christianity. This worried her parents. They thought that the Christians might influence their daughter. They decided to lock her, together with twelve maidservants, away in a tower. The parents also included images of their pagan god. But what they didn't know was that one of the maidservants was a Christian. She gladly told Christina about Jesus Christ, and by the time they were released Christina believed in the one true God.

When the time came for them to leave the tower, Christina smashed the images of the pagan god, much to the horror of her father. He beat her, and the servants, with rods, until their bodies bled. The next day he visited Christina. He was amazed to see there was no sign that she had suffered such a terrible beating. He was furious and ordered her to be tied to a wheel and set alight. As gigantic flames shot up, everyone around her was burnt, but Christina remained unharmed.

Her father was even angrier, and tied a millstone around her neck and threw her in the sea. However, before she could drown angels came and carried her safely to the shore. Her father's rage increased, he didn't know what more he could do. In desperation he ordered her to be killed with arrows. At last he succeeded in killing his daughter. He had tried to separate her from her Christian beliefs, but had managed to reunite her with the one true God.

Christina developed her faith in God through her friendship with others. Are your friendships keeping you close to God?

Chris, Chrissy, Christa, Christel, Christeta, Christiana, Christiane, Christianna, Christianne, Christin, Christine, Christo Christof, Christoffer, Christoph, Christophe, Chrystal, Cristiana, Cristina, Cristo, Cristoforo, Dina, Kersti, Kerstin, Kerstina, Kirsten, Kirstin, Kristin, Kristina,

JAMES THE GREAT

25 JULY

James and his brother John were two of the twelve apostles chosen by Jesus. Jesus had given James and his brother John the name 'Sons of Thunder', because both were men with fiery tempers. James was also known as, James the Great, because there was another younger apostle James. They were simple fishermen on Lake Galilee, and when Jesus invited them to leave their boats and follow him, they had no hesitation. They saw how he cared for the sick and the poor. They listened as he spread God's message. They shared his joys and sorrows.

After the death and resurrection of Jesus and the coming of the Holy Spirit, James spent his time telling the people of Jerusalem all he knew about Jesus. He was a great speaker and well respected amongst the people. They listened to him, and through him many came to believe in Jesus. His popularity came to the notice of King Herod Agrippa. He felt James was becoming too powerful, too dangerous. He felt the people were listening to James and not to him.

One day, as James was speaking to a great crowd, he was arrested. He was then condemned to death, and in the year 44 AD James was martyred. He was the first of the apostles to die. He had lost his life rather than lose his belief in Jesus.

Many years later his remains were taken to Santiago de Compostella in Spain. There, a new devotion to James began, and a scallop shell became its symbol. Thousands of Christian pilgrims visit his shrine. It has become the third largest place of pilgrimage after Rome and Jerusalem.

People were jealous of James because he became too popular. Why do you think some people are jealous of the popularity of others?

Diego, Giacomo, Hamish, Iacopo, Iago, Jack, Jacki, Jacob, Jacopo, Jacques, Jago, Jaime, Jakob, Jameson, Jamie, Jan, Jay, Jim, Jimbo, Jimi, Jimmie, Jimmy, Santiago, Seamus, Shamus, Sheamus

73

ANNE AND

26 JULY

Anne and Joachim were a devoted couple. Like many other devout people, at that time, they believed that the promised Messiah would come to bring salvation to all. They loved each other dearly, but sadly after twenty years of marriage they were still childless. They longed for a child, but accepted God's will. One day something quite extraordinary happened that would change their lives forever.

Joachim was in the desert and Anne was at home, when an angel appeared to both of them at the same time. The angel told them that they would soon have a child, a very special child. Immediately they went to the temple to thank God for this great news.

They arrived at the gate at the same time and fell joyously into each other's arms. Together, they went inside and knelt before God, and humbly thanked him for his wonderful gift. Some time later Anne gave birth to a little girl and they named her Mary. This very special couple had been chosen as the parents of a child who would become the mother of Jesus, the long awaited Messiah.

When she was still very young they took Mary back to the temple to present her to God. Mary immediately ran up the steps, eager to be in God's presence. It was as if she knew that this was where she belonged. Mary stayed with her parents until, as a young woman, she left them to be with Joseph and to give birth to Jesus. She often brought Jesus to see them, and they thanked God for the many blessings he had given them.

Joachim

Today, images of Anne are of a mother with her loving daughter. Because Anne never gave up hope of having a child, she has become the patron saint of childless women. Joachim also has a special place in the hearts of many, as the protector of married couples.

Anne and Joachim were parents who were close to God. Do you pray for your parents and ask God to bless them?

Anna, Anette, Ania, Anika, Anita, Ann, Annette, Anni, Annika, Annuschka, Hanna, Hannah, Nan, Nancy, Nanette, Nanine, Netta

Achim, Akim, Gioacchino, Joakim, Joaquin, Jochem, Jochen, Jochim, Jokum, Kim

IGNATIUS OF LOYOLA

31 JULY

As a teenager Inigo, as he was then called, was quite badly behaved. When he grew up he decided on a life in the military and became an officer. During a battle he was badly injured and his recovery was long and slow. He was bored. One day, someone brought him a few books to read. His excitement at receiving something to pass the time, soon turned to annoyance when he realised the books were about the lives of saints. When he finally started to read the books, he was deeply moved by what they contained. It made him think about his own life, and the sort of person he had become. Now he was ashamed. He had wasted too many years.

When he recovered from his injuries he retreated to a cave. He wanted to be alone with his thoughts. He hardly slept, and ate very little. He wore only a few clothes, even on the coldest days. He spent his time praying as a penance for the wrongs he had done. He had left his busy life and now had time to think. Gradually he began to put his thoughts and ideas into a little notebook. He decided to start a religious order that would make God's name even better understood on earth. He moved to Paris, and studied at the university in preparation for his plans. He was now known as Ignatius. A few men, who were enthusiastic about his ideas, joined him. They decided to call the order the Jesuits.

Soon more and more men joined, and it wasn't long before the Jesuits numbered several hundred. At that time most of the religious orders lived in monasteries, but the Jesuits were different. Their work was in hospitals, schools and universities. It was not long before the first Jesuits travelled to India as missionaries, bringing them the good news of Jesus. In time, Jesuit communities were established in many parts of the world.

Ignatius had worked long and hard achieving his dream and died in 1556. From a small notebook in a cave, the Jesuits had spread God's message far and wide. Today, children throughout the world owe their excellent education to the work of Ignatius and the Jesuit order.

> When he read about the lives of saints, Ignatius changed his own life. Which saint in this book inspires you the most?

Egnatius, Hynek, Ignacio, Ignatij, Ignatz, Ignaz, Ignazio, Inigo, Naze

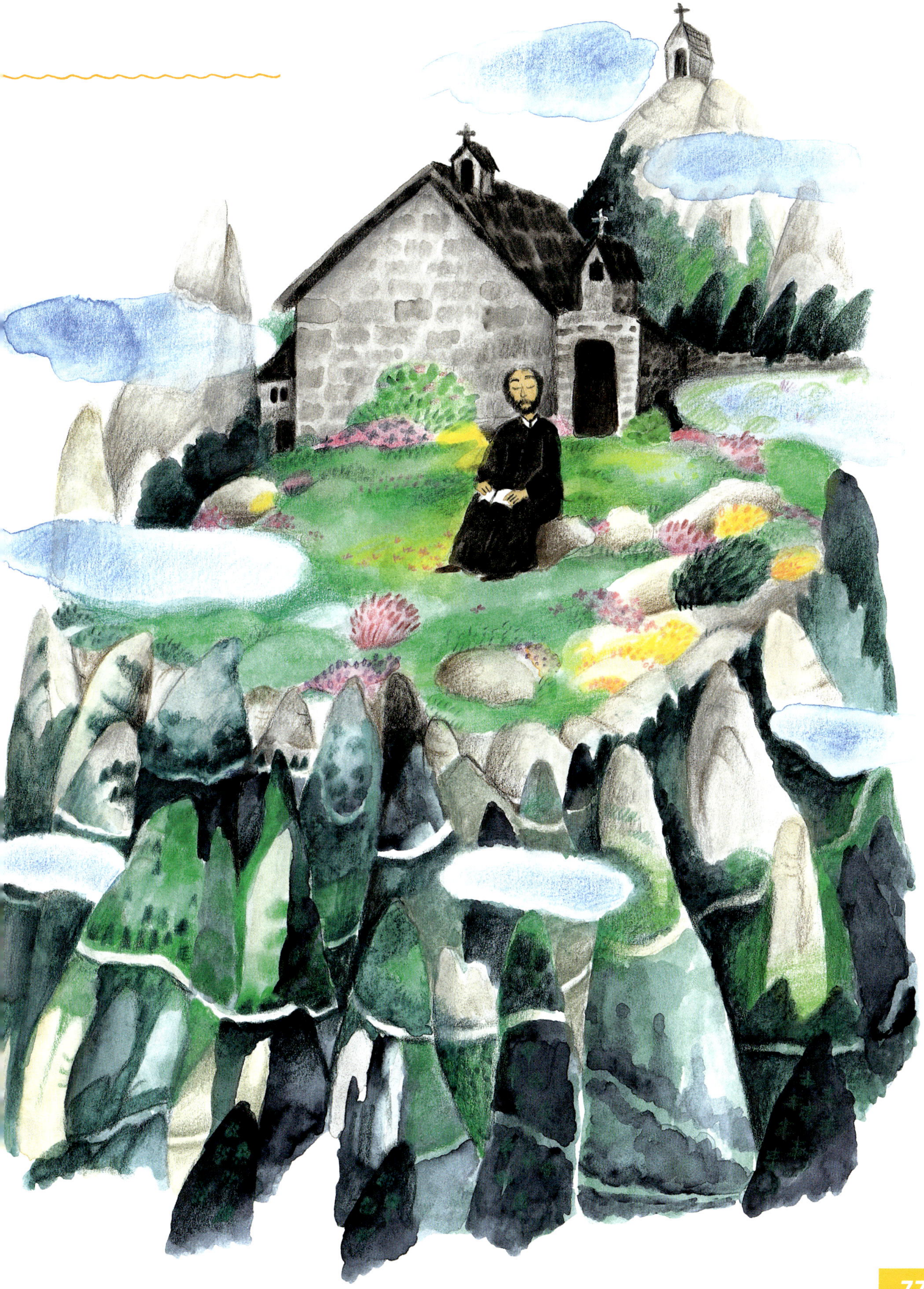

8 AUGUST

DOMINIC

In the year 1170, a few days before Dominic was born, Dominic's mother had a frightening dream. She dreamt that the child in her womb was a small dog who was carrying a burning torch in his mouth. As she gave birth, the dog used the torch to set the whole world alight. She was upset by this, and didn't realise that in the distant future the true meaning of the dream would become clear.

In time, she gave birth to a healthy boy. As he grew she became aware of his great intelligence. At university he studied theology and philosophy, and made a deep impression on all those who met him. It was not only his distinctive auburn hair that made him stand out from the crowd, but his love and devotion to God. But Dominic was troubled. All the debates, which took place in the university, seemed so remote from what was happening in the Church at that time. There was too much emphasis on ceremony and wealth. More and more people were rejecting the Church and its beliefs.

Dominic wanted to do something about it. He began travelling around villages, preaching and praying with the people. He listened to them and discussed their concerns. Gradually, with their faith rekindled, they returned to the Church. Dominic successfully continued his work for many years, travelling throughout Spain, France and Italy.

Soon, Dominic had more and more followers and in 1215 the Dominican religious order was formed. The pope quickly recognised the success of this different approach to spreading God's message. He asked Dominic to establish his order as quickly as possible in other countries. He knew that this humble man from Spain would help to renew the Church in this difficult period in its history.

Tired and weary from his work, Dominic died in year 1221. Today, the example set by Dominic has continued throughout the world. The true meaning of his mother's dream was now apparent. Her son had lit up the world with his teachings and ministry.

? Dominic changed the world by the way he talked to people about God. How can you talk to people to change your world for the better?

Doman, Domenico, Domingo, Dominicus, Dominik, Dominique, Dunko, Kus

LAURENCE

10 AUGUST

Images of Laurence show him holding a gridiron in his hand. According to legend he was martyred by being roasted over a gridiron.

Laurence was a young deacon, who came from Spain to Rome and worked with Pope Sixtus II. At that time, the Roman Emperor Valerian ruled over the Empire. He was a pagan. He hated the Christians and was notorious for persecuting them. Valerian did not even respect the pope. He sent his soldiers to capture and execute him while he was preaching in church. Valerian then summoned Laurence and asked him to hand over all the Church property to him. Laurence quietly replied,
"Yes the Church possesses many precious treasures. Give me three days and I will bring these treasures to you."

Punctually, after three days, Laurence returned to present the Church's treasures to the Emperor Valerian. He brought before the Emperor the poor people, the crippled people, and the outcasts of the city. Laurence proudly declared to the Emperor,
"These are the great treasures of the Church. They are more precious than all the gold in the world. They are the Church's brightest diamonds."

Valerian was beside himself with fury. This young deacon had made him look a fool. He instructed his soldiers to kill Laurence immediately.

They chose a particularly slow form of death. They tied Laurence to a gridiron and slowly roasted him over a fire. Not once did Laurence complain. He quietly prayed and faced his death with great courage.

> Laurence reminded the Emperor that people are more important than things. How do you put people before things in your life?

Enz, Enzeli, Lars, Lasse, Laure, Laurens, Laurent, Laurenz, Lauri, Laurids, Laurin, Laurits, Lauritz, Lauro, Laurus Lawrence, Lorenz, Lorenzino, Lorenzo, Loris, Renz, Renzo, Rienzo

CLARE OF ASSISI

When Clare was a young girl she was a friend of Francis of Assisi. They were like brother and sister and would spend hours in each other's company.

But there was a time when Clare rarely saw him. He travelled around the country preaching and baptising people. Clare missed him. Once, she asked him when he would be visiting Assisi again. He replied,
"When the roses are in bloom."
This made Clare even more unhappy. It was deep winter and not the time for flowers to bloom. Suddenly, she couldn't believe her eyes. All around her, beautiful roses started to flower. This miracle affected Clare deeply, and she decided to leave home. Her family was wealthy, but she no longer wanted to be surrounded by riches. She wanted to devote her life to Christ.

When her parents saw her again they were shocked by her appearance. She had shaved her hair and wore a plain, simple dress. Together with several companions, she travelled around the country preaching and telling people about Christ. Later, they retreated to the San Damiano convent and called themselves the Poor Clares. There they lived a life of poverty and prayer. Clare looked after her companions, and it's even been said that, although she was the superior in the convent, it was she who served the sisters. When Clare died in the year 1253, after a very painful illness, there were already over one hundred and fifty Poor Clare convents throughout Europe. This religious order, devoted to poverty and service, is now known throughout the world.

Clare and Francis encouraged each other to be good and God blessed their friendship. How could you encourage your friends to be good?

Chiara, Claire, Clairette, Clara, Clará, Clarice, Clarina, Clarinda, Clarissa, Clarita, Klarissa

MAXIMILIAN KOLBE

14 AUGUST

The story of Maximilian Kolbe, and the events that led up to his death, is still an inspiration to people today. He was born Raymond Kolbe in Poland in 1894. He studied in Rome, and was ordained in the Franciscan order, taking the name Maximilian. His health was poor, but it did not prevent him from dedicating himself to his priestly duties. He was also committed to establishing a devotion to Our Blessed Lady, and successfully published Catholic newspapers, both in Poland and Japan.

When the Second World War broke out in 1939, German soldiers stationed near his home in Poland, stopped him from publishing his newspapers. They went even further and arrested him. He was put into a striped prison uniform, and given a number – 16670. They transported him to Auschwitz prison camp.

When he arrived there, he was shocked by what he saw. Men, women and children were dressed in similar prison garb. They were crowded into huts. The conditions were inhuman and they were frightened and bewildered. He was angry. He wanted to do something. He wanted to speak up for these people, but what could he do? He decided that the best way was to be there for them, to share in their pain and to comfort them with God's word.

One day something terrible happened. Some of the prisoners were working in the field when one of them escaped. The commandant of the prison was furious. He cruelly decided that the loss of one man would be punished by the death of ten men. The men were chosen at random. One of them, a family man called Francis Gajowniczek broke down and cried. He was heartbroken. His wife and children needed him. Who would look after them when he was gone? Who would protect them? Maximilian heard him crying, and his heart went out to him. He stepped forward and in a strong voice said,

"I will die in his place."

Everyone looked shocked, including the commandant. It didn't matter to him who was chosen. So Maximilian replaced Francis, and all ten of them were lead away and put into a darkened bunker. They were given no food. Maximilian tried to keep their spirits high and urged them not to despair. They were heard singing and talking. Not once did anyone hear a word of complaint. One by one they died of hunger and exhaustion.

Maximilian allowed a prisoner to be free by taking his place.
How can you help your friends to be free of pressure or sadness?

Massimiliano, Massimilien, Massiminiano, Massimino, Massimo, Max, Maxence, Maxim, Maxime, Maximian, Maximianus, Maximilien, Maximin, Maximinian, Maximinianus, Maximinus

Finally, only Maximilian was left. He was just skin and bones. He was so weak he could not stand or walk. The commandant gave the order and he was shot dead. It was 14th August 1941 and Maximilian Kolbe was just 47 years old. When the prisoners of Auschwitz heard of his death, everyone prayed for the courageous priest, who had given his life to save the family man Francis Gajowniczek.

Forty-one years later, in St Peter's Basilica in Rome, Pope John Paul II canonised Maximilian Kolbe. Those attending the ceremony were deeply moved by the sight of an elderly man sitting with his wife, crying bitterly. He was dressed in a simple black suit. The man was Francis Gajowniczek.

BERNARD OF CLAIRVAUX

Bernard's mother died when he was still very young. He had been born in a palace in the year 1090, the son of wealthy parents. His mother's death had a profound effect on him. He decided now was the time to change his life radically. He wanted to leave behind the riches of the palace and devote his life to God, so he entered a Cistercian monastery.

Bernard was soon recognised by the abbot as being someone very special. He was a deeply spiritual person and seemed to be able to share his spirituality with others. He was an exceptional preacher and his reputation spread far and wide. People came from the surrounding countryside just to hear him preach.

Many were so moved by his sermons, they remained at the monastery, and eventually joined the Cistercian order.

Bernard was given the task of building a new monastery in a nearby forest. Following the example of Jesus, he chose twelve 'apostles' to help him. Using only their hands they cleared the forest, chopping down trees and using the wood to build the monastery. Their hands became rough and sore. They hardly slept and ate only what they could find in the forest. Finally the new monastery was finished.

Everyone was full of admiration for what he had achieved. They recognised his work, his inspirational sermons and the strength of his character. He had made a lasting impression on important people in society, including bishops and the pope. Many valued his friendship and appreciated his advice. Later, when the sacred city of Jerusalem was being attacked by the Saracens, they wanted Bernard to lead the crusade.

Sadly, it was not a success. The crusade failed and Bernard returned to the monastery bitterly disappointed. He retreated to his cell and his health began to fail. On 20th August 1153, completely exhausted, he died surrounded by the monks who had loved and respected him, as a teacher and as a friend.

People really listened to what Bernard had to say. How important is it for you to really listen to others?

Barney, Benno, Benso, Berend, Bernardin, Bernardino, Bernardo, Berney, Bernhardin, Bernie, Berno, Bernt, Bero

BARTHOLOMEW

24 AUGUST

Bartholomew became an apostle in a most unusual way. One day he met his friend Philip, who was already an apostle. Philip said to him,
"We've found the Messiah. It is Jesus, the son of Joseph of Nazareth. Why don't you come and see him?"
Bartholomew, who used to be called Nathaniel, answered him rather sarcastically,
"Can anything good come from a place like Nazareth?"
However Bartholomew became curious and decided to go along and find out for himself.

As soon as they were introduced, Jesus told Bartholomew he recognised his honesty and integrity. This compliment from Jesus made a deep impression on Bartholomew. When Jesus asked him to become one of his apostles he readily agreed. From that day on, Bartholomew remained faithfully at his side. Bartholomew was often called the happy apostle. It was he who settled heated squabbles between the apostles, with kind words and a cheery smile.

After the crucifixion and resurrection of Jesus, Bartholomew undertook several difficult mission trips. He covered thousand of miles, often on foot or on a donkey. He travelled to India, Egypt and Asia Minor. He spread the good news of Jesus everywhere he went. The manner of his death is uncertain. Some people say he was beheaded.

Others say he was flayed alive and crucified, head downward. In the painting of the Last Judgement by Michelangelo, which is in the Vatican in Rome, Bartholomew is represented as holding his skin in his hand, indicating that he was flayed alive.

> Bartholomew was able to make peace between the apostles. How can you bring peace to others when there are arguments?

Bart, Bartel, Barthel, Bartho, Bartholomé, Bartolomeo

LOUIS

25 AUGUST

King Louis IX was a kind and just man. It has been said that he was a perfect king and an example to other royals. His father died when he was just eleven years old. As successor to his father, he was crowned King of France. It was a difficult time for him but with his mother's advice and guidance he succeeded. Although he was very young, he was popular with the people. They could not wish for a better king.

Whilst he was still young he married Margaret. The southern part of France belonged to her family and their marriage meant France was now united. They eventually had eleven children, and they enjoyed a happy family life. Other kings decorated themselves with fine clothes and jewellery, but Louis lived humbly. Every day at noon, together with his family, he attended a service in church. He ate with the poor outside the palace gate and cared for them. He visited the hospitals, comforting the sick. He built schools and universities from his own money so that everyone had an education. He considered his kingship to be a gift from God.

When he heard that the Saracens had conquered the city of Jerusalem, he called together many men to lead a crusade to free the city. However, after six years they failed and returned to France. But Louis didn't give up hope and soon made another attempt. Sadly, on the journey to Jerusalem, Louis became ill. An epidemic had broken out on the ship and Louis tragically died.

When news of his death reached France the whole of the country mourned. People wept in the streets, they had lost a great king and a true friend.

Louis was a king who chose to be with people who had nothing. How could you help people who do not have many friends?

Gigio, Gino, Lajos, Lewis, Lodovico, Lois, Lotz, Lovis, Lowik, Ludewig, Ludovic, Ludovico, Ludovicus, Ludvik, Luigi, Luis, Lutz

AUGUSTINE

28 AUGUST

All mothers worry about their children and Monica was no exception. She lived in North Africa and her son Augustine was born in the year 354 AD. He was bright and intelligent and left home for university at a very young age. Sometime later when Monica visited her son, she couldn't believe her eyes. He was only sixteen and yet he was living with his girlfriend and they had a son Adeodatus. His lifestyle was wild and he cared little about anyone but himself. Monica was shocked and deeply upset both by the appearance of her son and by his behaviour. She pleaded with him, time and time again, to change. This only made Augustine more defiant than ever.

He loved his mother dearly but was unable to stand it any longer, and moved to Italy with his girlfriend and Adeodatus. However, Monica didn't give up and resolutely followed him. She begged him to change his ways. She prayed that Jesus would help him to see how his behaviour was damaging himself and those around him. Although the pleas of his mother touched his heart, he still refused to change.

Monica never gave up hope, she continued to pray for her son. It was many years later when her prayers were finally answered. Augustine read something that had a profound effect on him. In one of his letters, St Paul had written that salvation was not through arguments and disputes, nor excesses, but through Jesus Christ. Augustine thought carefully about what he had read. Gradually it became clear and he realised what he must do. He asked his respected teacher, Ambrose of Milan, to baptise both him and his son Adeodatus. He made the decision that from now on his life would be very different. He put his past behind him and moved back to North Africa.

Once there, he devoted his life to Christ. He became a priest and later Bishop of Hippo. He founded the Augustinian religious order and wrote many influential books. He was dedicated to his work and the people respected and trusted him. After a long and eventful life he died on 28th August in the year 430 AD.

Augustine was helped to make sense of his life through the prayers of his Mother. Who do you need to keep in your prayers?

Agost, Agostino, Agosto, Agoston, Augst, August, Augustin, Augusto, Augustus, Austin, Gus, Gust, Gustel

8 SEPTEMBER

MARY

Mary the mother of Jesus has a special place in our hearts. She is seen as the mother of us all. Many people have a devotion to Mary and pray to her for help in their time of need. Mary's feast days are celebrated throughout the year, but it is September 8th, her birthday, which is so special.

Mary's parents were Anne and Joachim. They had longed for a child, but after twenty years of marriage they were still childless. They had almost given up hope, when an angel appeared and told them they would soon have a daughter and she would be named Mary. They soon realised she was very special and she brought them great joy. She grew into a beautiful young woman and later became engaged to Joseph. He was a carpenter from Nazareth and was devoted to her.

One day something happened which would change Mary's life forever. The angel Gabriel appeared to Mary. He told her she was going to have a child who would be the long awaited Messiah. Mary didn't understand why she had been chosen, but trusted in God.

When Joseph heard the news, he was worried. He wasn't sure what the future would hold. Later, an angel appeared to him. He told Joseph that the child was a gift from God. This reassured Joseph. He knew that from now on he would care for Mary and the baby.

Mary loved and cared for the child Jesus. How can we help mothers to provide for their children in countries where there is so much poverty and hunger?

Mae, Maia, Maike, Maire, Maja, Mami, Manon, Marei, Maria, Mareike, Mareile, Marella, Maren, Mariana, Marica, Maricke, Marie, Marieka, Marieke, Mariella, Marietta, Marihuela, Marija, Marijke, Marike, Marilyn, Marinetta, Marinka, Marion, Maris, Mariska, Marita, Maritta, Marja, Marka, Maruscha, Maruska, Marya, Mascha, Maschinka, Maura, Maureen, May, Meike, Mia, Mieke, Mieze, Mimi, Minnie, Miriam, Mirjam, Mirl, Mitzi, Mizzi, Ria

Later, when it was getting near the time for Mary to give birth, they travelled to Bethlehem for a census. It was a long and difficult journey. When they arrived, the little town was crowded. Everyone had come for the census and they couldn't find anywhere to stay. Joseph was desperate and eventually accepted the shelter of a stable from a kindly innkeeper. That night Jesus was born. Later Mary and Joseph returned to Nazareth with Jesus where they lived happily as a family.

After the death of Joseph, Mary continued to care for her son Jesus. She remained with him throughout his life. She was there at the marriage feast at Cana and witnessed the miracle of the water and wine. She saw him give comfort to the poor, the sick and the lame. Mary listened as Jesus told people about God. Finally, she suffered a mother's pain when she watched as people shouted and jeered as he carried his heavy cross on the road to Calvary. She was there for him, standing at the foot of the cross when he died.

ROBERT BELLARMINE

17 SEPTEMBER

Soon after his university studies Robert Bellarmine was ordained a priest. He was a brilliant scholar who wanted to use his academic achievements in the service of God and the Church. The excellent reputation of this learned man spread across the whole of Europe. It was a time of confusion and unrest in the Church. Martin Luther had established a new movement, from which the Protestant Church developed, and Christians had begun to argue amongst themselves.

At this time the pope was looking for someone who would be able to define and explain doctrine, and lessen tension within the Church. It needed to be someone who was exceptionally knowledgeable about Church matters. News of Robert's knowledge and understanding of the Church reached the pope. He considered Robert to be an excellent choice as an ambassador for the Church.

Robert accepted the challenge and began to write. His learned documents were read and valued. It did much to strengthen the Church in many parts of Europe. He worked tirelessly, successfully producing important books and letters. He most famous work was the Bellarmine Catechism. This was later translated into sixty languages.

However, pressure of work took its toll. Robert's health began to deteriorate. As he grew weaker he was forced to work less and less. The pope respected this deeply spiritual man, and he was made a cardinal. After a long and fulfilling life Robert died in the year 1621. At a very young age he had vowed to use his talents in the service of the Church. His dedication and service is still remembered today.

> Robert was very clever and used this to help others to learn. What could you do to help other people to learn?

Bert, Bertes, Bob, Hob, Hodge, Rob, Robby, Robel, Robelin, Roberta, Roberto, Robertus, Robi, Robin, Robrecht, Rodebert, Rodebrecht, Rollo, Rupert, Rupertus,

Hildegard

Hildegard of Bingen was considered to be one of the wisest and cleverest women of her time. Now, over eight hundred years after her death, her teachings are still valued. She was a doctor, natural scientist and a politician and a composer of great music. She was born in the area around the River Rhine in 1098. As a young child she was sent to a convent to be educated. It was soon realised that Hildegard was a very exceptional child. Apart from her obvious intelligence, she had deep and meaningful conversations with God. They were never heard by anyone else, but Hildegard told a friend what God had told her, and her friend wrote them down. Even to the present day the work is known and read across the world.

When Hildegard grew to adulthood she became a nun, and eventually the abbess of the convent. She commented courageously on important political and social topics of the day. At that time, the behaviour of many in society, including religious leaders, was disgraceful. Many treated their staff badly and thought only of their own wealth and welfare. Hildegarde openly criticised them and as a result they made life very difficult for her.

She knew a great deal about natural medicine and healthy nutrition. She developed an abundant herb garden in the convent and used these natural plant ingredients in her recipes and cures. These are still used today, under the title 'Hildegard Medicine'.

She died in the convent on 17th September 1179. Not only had she devoted her life to God, but also by her cures, saved the lives of many people.

> Hildegard realised that her intelligence was a gift to be used for others. What gifts do you have and how can they be used to help others?

Hidda, Hilda, Hilde, Hildegarda, Hilke, Hilla

17 SEPTEMBER

STANISLAUS

In a famous painting of Stanislaus, he is shown as a young street urchin. His clothes are ragged and there is sadness in his big dark eyes. It was painted just before he died. Stanislaus Kostka was born in Poland in the year 1550. His family belonged to the Polish aristocracy.

When he was just eight years old he was sent to a famous Jesuit school in Vienna, together with his brother Paul. Stanislaus was a popular boy, always polite and a good friend to other students. He was also deeply spiritual and often heard the voice of Jesus. This caused Paul to mock him and laugh at him. He was jealous of his popular brother, and did all he could to humiliate him.

Paul's lifestyle at school was very different from his brother's. He had no time for lessons or prayers. At night he enjoyed visiting the city and having a good time. Stanislaus pretended to ignore the bullying and put on a brave face, but inwardly he was very hurt by Paul's actions. Paul's attitude upset Stanislaus, and in desperation he came to a decision. He told Paul that he would not be returning to the family home, and asked him to explain the reasons to his parents. He later asked to be received into the Jesuit order. However, it was thought that his father would not want this, and permission was refused.

Stanislaus was not deterred. He put on ragged clothes, and pulled a hat over his face so that he would not be recognised. He left Vienna and set out on a long and arduous walk. After one exhausting week on the road, he finally reached the Jesuit house in Bavaria. Peter Canisius, a famous Jesuit, who was impressed by his courage, kindly welcomed him. He advised Stanislaus to go to the Jesuit house in Rome.

Once more Stanislaus set out on a long and difficult journey. Whenever his spirits were low, he listened to the voice of Jesus and this gave him the will to carry on. When he finally arrived in Rome he was accepted as a novice in the Jesuit order, and his preparation for the priesthood began. Everyone marvelled at his bravery in reaching his goal. He became a popular student and a good example to all. However, the illness that had once afflicted him returned. He sensed that he would shortly die and prepared himself to meet God.

Just before the feast of the Assumption of Our Lady, his condition deteriorated. Stanislaus sat alone in his little room and wrote a letter to Our Lady. He asked to be united with her in heaven, so that they could share her feast day together. On the morning of the feast, 15th August 1568, Stanislaus died. He was just seventeen years old.

Stanislaus began his journey to holiness by ignoring bullying and achieving his dream. How can you make sure that what you say and do, does not make others feel bullied?

Stan, Stanel, Stanes, Stani, Stanislao, Stanislas, Stanislav, Stanislaw, Stanko, Stano, Stas, Stasch, Stenzel

MATTHEW

21 SEPTEMBER

When Matthew was invited by Jesus to join him as one of his apostles, it came as a great surprise. Many of the apostles already chosen were fishermen. They were simple hard-working men, who were known and loved by everyone in the community. But Matthew was different. He was a tax collector, and was known as Levi. He was not popular with the people, as it was his job to collect taxes for the treasury, and no one liked paying taxes. Everyone was shocked that he was chosen. Levi felt honoured that Jesus had faith in him. Despite Levi's reputation Jesus wanted him as his apostle. Jesus named him Matthew, which means 'the trusted one' or 'gift from God'.

He left behind his old life and the resentment of the people; he was now Matthew the apostle. From that day onwards, he travelled with Jesus and helped him to comfort the sick and help those in need. He prayed with him and shared in his joys and sadness.

Later, after the death and resurrection of Jesus, the apostles travelled far and wide spreading the Gospel message. Matthew went eastward to Mesopotamia, bringing the good news of Jesus Christ. After many years of preaching, and converting thousands to a belief in the one true God, he started to write about his time with Jesus.

This is how Matthew is remembered today, as an apostle and evangelist. His symbol is of a winged man. The Gospel he wrote is an important document in the Church, it was written by a man who was given a chance and found a new life in Jesus.

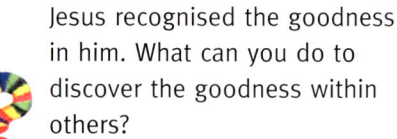

Matthew was not popular but Jesus recognised the goodness in him. What can you do to discover the goodness within others?

Mathias, Mattieu, Matheu, Matteo, Mattheis, Matthuas, Mathern, Mayhew, Mathew, Mattheson, Matthieson, Mattheus, Matt Matous · Mateusz · Matwei

Jonah

21 SEPTEMBER

Jonah lived about seven hundred and fifty years before the birth of Jesus. He had a very special talent; he was able to see into the future and was called a prophet. He used his powers to predict the fate of the people. One day, God asked him to visit the city of Nineveh. The citizens were not good people; they cared for no one but themselves, and were wasting their lives. God told Jonah that unless they changed their ways, their city would be destroyed within forty days. Jonah was reluctant to give this awful message to the people. He was scared of their reaction. He just couldn't face them. He decided to run away.

One night he quietly boarded a ship. He remained hidden and waited for it to set sail. Later, when the ship had left the harbour and reached the open sea a great storm broke out. It threatened to overturn the ship and the crew panicked. As soon as they discovered Jonah on board they blamed him for the storm, and they threw him overboard.

As he hit the water a giant whale swam past and opened his huge jaws. Jonah fell straight into his mouth, and with one large gulp, the whale swallowed him. Jonah looked around, he was now inside the fish. He was actually inside the fish's stomach. However, he didn't moan and groan about his misfortune but thanked God for rescuing him from drowning. For three days and three nights Jonah remained inside the whale. Finally, the whale spat him out.

Realising what he must now do, he travelled as fast as he could, back to Nineveh. He told the people they must change their ways, or something awful would happen to the city. The reaction of the citizens was unexpected. They didn't become aggressive, or shout or scream, but appeared to be very frightened. They realised their wrongdoings, and immediately changed their ways and the city was spared.

Later, God spoke to Jonah once more. He told him he should have trusted him. God knew the men, women and children would not die. He knew they would change their ways. Jonah now understood. He realised the importance of his work. He knew that he should always put his trust in God.

> Jonah found it difficult to do what was right. How can you try to do the right thing, even if it means making difficult decisions?

Giona, Jon, Jona, Gian, Gianni, Evan

26 SEPTEMBER

COSMAS & DAMIAN

The fourth century was a time when the rulers of the Roman Empire persecuted many Christians. Cosmas and Damian came from Syria. They were brothers, possibly twins, and had been baptised Christians. Both had chosen a career in medicine, and dedicated their lives to caring for the sick and making them well again. Not only did they treat the physical health of their patients, but they also told them about Jesus Christ.

It wasn't long before one of their patients told the Roman governor about their attempt to convert him to Christianity. Immediately he ordered their arrest. He threatened them with death unless they gave up their faith, but the brothers would not give in. They would rather die than reject Jesus. This made the governor even angrier and he ordered his soldiers to kill them.

When news of their death reached the people, they cried openly. Stories about the two brothers, who helped so many people, quickly spread. Long after their death, they were still mourned in many countries. Devotion to them grew, and there were religious processions in their honour. They mourned the loss of these wonderful brothers. Cosmas and Damian had given them not only their good health, but also the most precious gift of all, their belief in Jesus Christ

Cosmas and Damian helped those who were ill. How can you help others to feel better about themselves?

Côme, Cosimo, Cosme, Cosmo

Damien, Damiano, Damianu

VINCENT DE PAUL

27 SEPTEMBER

Vincent was born in France, and as a child worked on his parent's farm. When his schooling was over, he had only one ambition and that was to become a priest. His father was poor, but readily agreed to sell two oxen to pay for his son's studies.

After his ordination, he decided to move to Paris. He thought there would be more opportunities for success in the big city. As soon as he arrived he was shocked by what he found. Thousands lived in poverty, and no one cared. His heart went out to these people, and he decided to give them the help and support they badly needed.

Vincent worked hard and began by enlisting the help of others. He set up a relief organisation, helping prisoners who were living in awful conditions. Next it was the turn of the beggars and homeless. They were given a free meal every day and the care and attention they needed.

The work was difficult but there was still more to be done. The number of babies abandoned on the streets distressed Vincent. Their mothers were desperate and too poor to keep them. He enrolled the help of trusted women to care for the children. Later they formed themselves into a religious order, called the Sisters of Charity.

Vincent dedicated the rest of his life to helping the poor, the disabled and anyone who needed his support. He asked for no reward, and said the look of gratitude in their eyes was enough for him. Vincent died in the year 1660 aged eighty. He is still remembered today, and the excellent charitable work of the Society of St Vincent de Paul continues.

> Vincent became a saint by helping people in practical ways. How can you give practical help to someone in need?

Vicente, Vicenzio, Vincentius, Vincenty, Vincenz, Vincenzo, Vinnie, Vinny, Vinz, Vinzent

WENCESLAUS

28 SEPTEMBER

In Prague, the capital of the Czech Republic there is a beautiful place called Wenceslaus Square. The country was once called Bohemia and this is where Wenceslaus was born in the year 907 AD. He was the son of a king, and at an early age lived with his grandmother. His father and grandmother were Christians, at a time when Christianity was not widespread in Bohemia. His grandmother educated Wenceslaus in the Christian faith, which angered his mother, who did not believe in Christ.

When Wenceslaus was about fifteen years old his father died. Although he was his father's rightful heir, he was too young to become king, and his mother took over the reign. She immediately expelled priests from the country, and destroyed the beautiful churches. She argued with her mother-in-law and had her murdered.

The people were furious. They rose up against her and she was expelled from the country.

Wenceslaus took his rightful place on the throne. He brought back the priests and rebuilt the churches. He was a fair and just ruler, which made him popular with the people.

During the next few years thousands of people in Bohemia converted to Christianity.

However, his mother's hatred continued in exile. Together with her second son Boleslav, she plotted revenge. When Wenceslaus was just twenty-eight years old, he visited Boleslav. His brother seized his opportunity to attack Wenceslaus. He crept up behind him and using a mighty sword stabbed him in the back. The people were devastated by his death. They had lost not only a fair and just ruler, they had also lost a friend.

Wenceslaus was a fair and just king. How can you be sure you are always fair and a good friend to others?

Ceslaus, Ceslav, Vaceslav, Vaclav, Venceslao, Venceslav, Wazlaw, Wenzeslaus, Wjatscheslaw

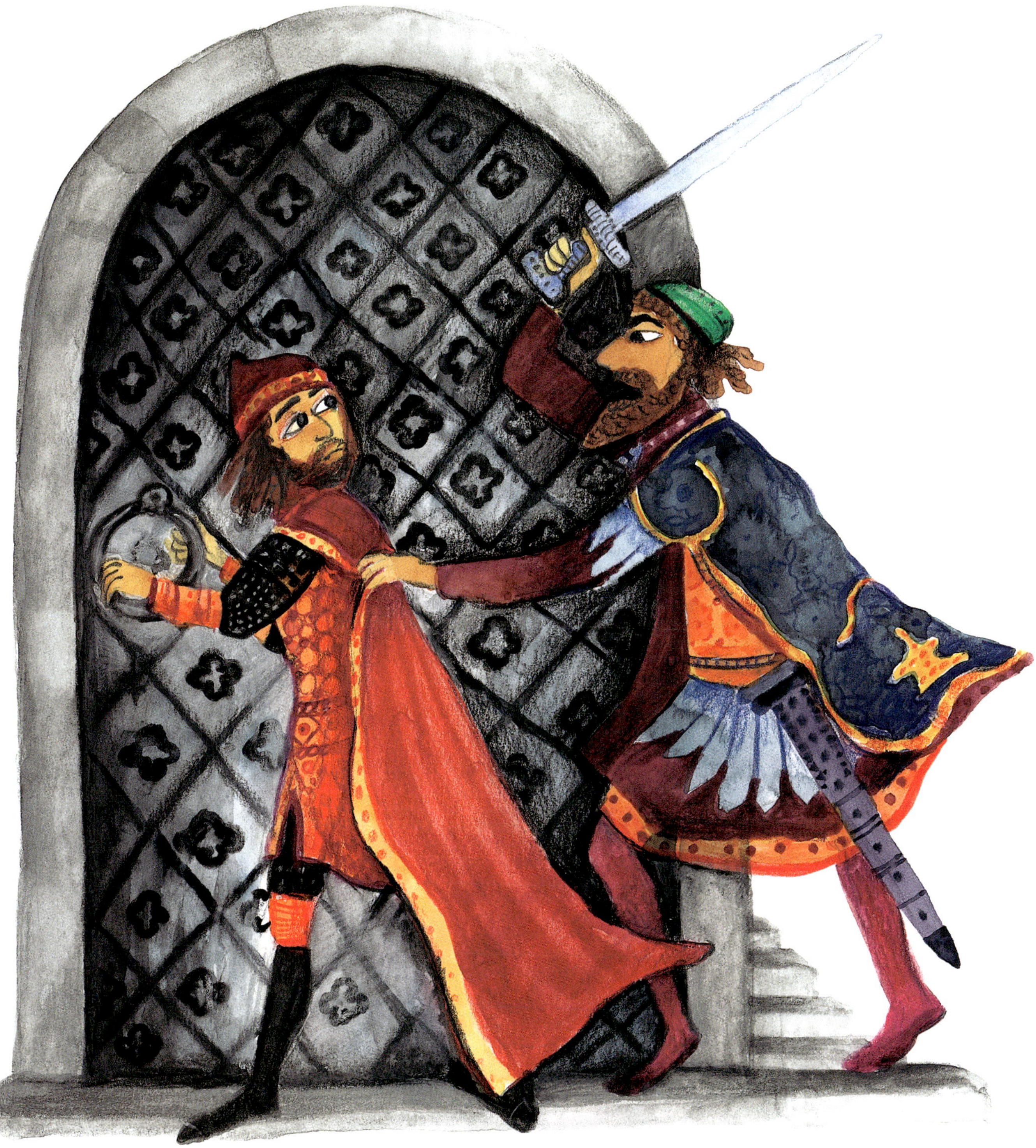

29 SEPTEMBER

MICHAEL

It has always been believed that angels bring messages from God. The more important angels are known as archangels, and the best known of these is Michael. He appears again and again in the Bible stories, particularly in crucial situations. It is the archangel Michael who watches over us, and takes our prayers to God.

Michael has many titles, indicating the way he has helped us. Such titles as, the loyal companion of the soul, the comforter of those in distress, the mediator between God and the human race.

He is even known as the protector of all God's people. It is said that he welcomes us to heaven when we die. Because he is so powerful and mighty, he can be considered as our great hero. The Bible tells us that it was he, who defeated the devil.

Many churches and mountain chapels are dedicated to Michael. In France, there is a famous shrine dedicated to St Michael. It is a place of pilgrimage. Mont-St-Michel is situated on the Atlantic coast of France. There is a similar island off the coast of Cornwall called St Michael's Mount.

The name Michael is very popular. It comes from the Hebrew language, which is the language of the people of Israel. It means, 'Who is like God'. Michaelmas Day is one of the quarter days, because it is when quarterly rent is due. Many universities call the first term of the year, Michaelmas, because students begin their studies on or around the 29th September.

> Michael is known as the protector of God's people. How can you protect those who need your help?

Micha, Michaelis, Michail, Michal, Michel, Michele, Michi, Michiel, Mick, Mickel, Miguel, Mikael, Mike, Minja, Mischa

GABRIEL

29 SEPTEMBER

Gabriel, the archangel is the bringer of good news. The name means 'man of God'. It was the Archangel Gabriel who appeared to Zechariah and Elizabeth. They had no children, and were both very old. When Zechariah saw the angel, he was surprised and afraid. But the angel said,
"Do not be afraid, Zechariah. God has heard your prayers. Your wife Elizabeth will have a son. He will be called John. He will bring you much joy."
Later, Zechariah and Elizabeth had a son and he was called John the Baptist.

Shortly after Elizabeth and Zechariah had received the good news, Gabriel appeared to Mary. She was engaged to Joseph, and Gabriel told her,
"You are going to have a son, who will be the Messiah. He will be named Jesus."
Mary didn't understand God's message. How could she be the mother of the Messiah? Gabriel said to her,
"With God, all things are possible."
Mary trusted in God and accepted this great honour. She became the mother of Jesus.

Gabriel is remembered today as the patron of all those who bring news to other people. The archangel Gabriel is regarded as the patron saint of messengers, journalists, and other members of the media, such as those who work in television, radio and newspapers.

Gabriel is considered as the patron saint of members of the media. How can the media help to make the world a better place?

Gábor, Gabriele, Gabriello, Gabrio, Gawril

29 SEPTEMBER

RAPHAEL

Raphael is the guardian and healer among the archangels. His name means 'God heals'. We read in the Old Testament that he came to the help of a family who lived in a city called Nineveh. The father of the family was a man called Tobit. He was blind and badly needed the return of some money he had lent to a friend, who lived a good distance from their home. He asked his son Tobias, to go and collect the money. As Tobias left the house, he found Raphael standing there, who offered to accompany him.

The archangel and the young man set off on their journey. It was long and tiring, so they stopped for the night by the side of the river Tigris. Tobias went down to the river to wash. Suddenly, a giant fish leapt out of the water. Raphael quickly came to the aid of Tobias, and helped him to kill the fish. They ate some of the fish for supper, but put aside the fish's heart, liver and gall. The archangel said they would need them later.

When they returned, the aged Tobit ran out to greet his son. He cried tears of joy at his safe return. His only sorrow was, that because of his blindness, he couldn't see his son's face. Raphael told Tobias to make a paste of the fish's gall and put it on his father's eyes. Miraculously, Tobit could see. Joyously they all thanked and praised God. Quietly the archangel Raphael left them. The task was over. Raphael had protected Tobias on his journey, and had restored Tobit's sight.

When some people narrowly miss having an accident they often say,
"My guardian angel must have been looking after me."

Raphael looked after Tobit and his family. When have you felt your guardian angel was helping you to make the right choice?

Raffael, Raffaele, Raffaello, Raffaelo, Rafail

THERESA OF LISIEUX

1 OCTOBER

Theresa was born in France in 1873. Sadly, when she was just five years old, her mother died. From that day onwards Theresa had little time for toys and play. Instead she spent her time helping her sisters, cooking, cleaning and generally taking care of the home.

She was a deeply spiritual child, and as she grew, she spent a great deal of her spare time in prayer and talking to God. This brought her an inner peace. She knew that anything she achieved in the future would be with God's help. As a teenager she travelled to Rome for a private meeting with the pope. Although she was very young she asked his permission to become a nun. He eventually granted her request and she soon settled into her new home, the Carmelite convent in Lisieux.

At first she was not treated kindly. They had never met anyone like Theresa. But her deep love of God was an example to everyone that knew her, and they soon realised Theresa was special. She often told others that we were like little children and our relationship with God was like that of a small child with our father.

Theresa suffered with tuberculosis and died in 1897 at just twenty-four years old. After her death a book was published from her diaries, called 'The Story of a Soul' describing her 'Little Way' of loving God. It was translated into thirty-five languages and still read by many people around the world. Theresa of Lisieux is one of the patron saints of the missions. Unlike many other great saints, she did not become a missionary, but supported them with her letters and prayers.

Theresa realised that God was close to her in the little things and ordinary feelings of every day. How can you make God close to you in all the ordinary events in your life?

Resa, Resi, Resia, Teresa, Terezie, Terka, Tess, Tessa, Thea, Theresina, Thery, Thesi, Tracy

4 OCTOBER — FRANCIS OF ASSISI

Like a sun, he shone upon our world. A famous Italian poet named Dante wrote these beautiful words. He was referring to Francis of Assisi. When the sun shines on us we feel good and this is the same effect Francis had on anyone who met him. They immediately sensed something very special about Francis, which made them feel good about themselves.

Francis was born in Assisi in Italy in the year 1181 or 1182, the exact year is uncertain. His father Peter Bernardone was a wealthy cloth merchant. His mother, Joanna Pica, belonged to a noble family from France. Francis was one of several children. At Baptism he received the name of John. His father later altered it to Francis. It would appear this was because his wife loved the country of her birth.

As a young man Francis loved pleasure; he enjoyed life, had a ready wit, a good voice for singing and spent money on fine clothes. When he was about twenty, Francis joined the army and had to fight against the soldiers from a neighbouring town. He was captured in battle and spent a year in prison. He contracted a fever and it seems that during a long illness his thoughts turned to more serious matters. He thought about the purpose of his life and how empty it had been up to then.

After a short period of uncertainty, he began to seek the answer in prayer and solitude. He had already given up his expensive clothes and wasteful ways, but he was not sure what he should do. He didn't know which way to turn. One morning he went to the chapel. The Gospel of the day told how the disciples of Christ were to possess neither gold nor silver, nor two coats, nor shoes, nor a staff. Francis felt as if these words were meant for him. He now knew what he must do. He gave all his clothes away to the poor, and became poor himself. He wore a brown woollen tunic, similar to the clothes worn by the poorest peasants, and tied a knotted rope around his waist.

Francis soon had many followers wearing the same brown tunic and hood and wearing sandals on their feet. They accepted his ideal of living as poor people, and serving only God. They were mendicants, the name given to poor men who live by begging. After the death of Francis his followers became known as Franciscans. They were missionaries preaching first in Italy, then throughout Europe and finally all over the whole world. Soon woman joined this movement. Clare of Assisi, who was a great childhood friend of Francis, established the order of the Poor Clares, enabling women to live in convents and work for God.

Francis of Assisi not only had a great love of people but he was devoted to the welfare of animals. He called them 'my brothers and sisters', and he seemed to be able to talk to them. He was often seen on the shore of a lake, talking to the fish, or perhaps on a hill speaking to the birds. Francis, in his beautiful 'Canticle of the Sun', described his love of nature and of all God's creatures. It still has the power to move people's hearts today.

Francis spent so much time and energy showing his concern for people, that he became completely exhausted. He died at the age of forty-four, on 3rd October 1226. His ideals and the Franciscans he founded, are still a source of inspiration in our world today.

> Francis saw God in animals, flowers and sunshine. Where do you see God in creation?

Ferenc, Franc, Francesco, Francisco, Francisk, Francisque, Franciszek, Franco, Francois, Franek, Franjo, Frank, Frans, Frantz

FAUSTINA KOWALSKA

5 OCTOBER

A few weeks before her twentieth birthday, Faustina heard a voice telling her that her future home would be in a convent. Later she heard the voice once more, but this time it was different. In front of her she saw a vision of Christ. She saw him suffering on the cross, and she knew she couldn't waste any more time, she knew what she must do. She promptly left home for Warsaw and entered a convent.

She had been born in Poland in 1905 of poor parents, and was given the name Helena. In order to help her family she obtained work as a maid. Later, in Warsaw, she settled down to a convent life of prayer and service to others, and took the name of Mary Faustina.

Faustina often heard the voice of Mary, the mother of Jesus. She continued to see visions of Jesus on the cross. It was during these visions that Jesus asked her to tell everyone about his Divine Mercy. He also asked her to write down what was in her heart, and all that she saw and heard during these visions. Later, the book about her thoughts was published and widely read.

Everyone began to realise Faustina was special. Whenever she met anyone she seemed to be able to see into their very soul, and was able to predict the future. Mary Faustina Kowalska died, aged thirty-three, on 5th October 1938, and the devotion to the Divine Mercy of Jesus continues to this day.

Faustina shared with others feelings that were in her heart. In what way could you open your heart to others?

Fausta, Faustine, Faustyna

SARAH

9 OCTOBER

The story of Sarah and her family can be found in the Old Testament. Sarah lived with her husband Abraham. They lived many years before the birth of Jesus. They were very happy together. Sarah was very beautiful and her husband loved her dearly.

God told Abraham that he would make him the father of all nations, but sadly Sarah remained childless. For decades they waited. Finally Sarah made a most difficult decision. She loved Abraham so much and knew how desperately he wanted a child. She told him to have a child with her maidservant Hagar. This arrangement was not uncommon at this time. Abraham consented with a heavy heart. He wanted to fulfil God's prophecy, but he loved Sarah. In time Hagar bore him a son and he was called Ishmael.

Some years passed and Abraham received another message from God. He told Abraham that Sarah would soon have a son, and all nations would come from her. Sarah could hardly believe it.

They were both already quite elderly and couldn't understand how they could have a child in their old age. Later, exactly as God had foretold, Sarah had a son and he was named Isaac. When Isaac grew into adulthood he too had a son called Jacob.

Sarah waited and trusted in God for what she wanted. How patient and trusting are you?

Sally, Sarah, Sarei, Sarina, Zara, Zarah

9 OCTOBER

DENIS

People are often startled when they see pictures or statues of Denis, because he his headless. Furthermore, he is holding his severed head in his hands. He lived in France in the third century and was consecrated as a bishop.

The pope at that time was Fabian. He sent Denis to Paris to take Christianity to the people. Once there, Denis preached to them and told them about Jesus. He was a kind and sincere man, and soon many were asking to be baptised. But there were still some who hated the Christians. When news of his conversions spread around the country, his enemies wanted him out of the way. They planned to kill him.

These people formed a group to look for him and to carry out the awful deed. However, as soon as they saw Denis and listened to him, they were impressed by his kindness, and found it difficult to go ahead with their plans. When the Roman governor heard this, he was furious. He immediately sent men to capture Denis and to take him to a hill above the city. There he was beheaded.

It is said that after his beheading, Denis, who seemed to be surrounded by a heavenly light, stood up. He then proceeded to take his severed head to the city. He did not stop until he reached the spot where he wanted to be buried. The place where Denis was beheaded became known as the Mountain of Martyrs. It is situated in the area of Paris, known as Montmartre.

Today many people in France have a great devotion to Denis. He is often asked for help from people who suffer with headaches or migraine.

People became Christian because they saw the goodness of Dennis.
Do you always let people see the goodness in you?

Denes, Dennis, Denys, Dinnies, Dins, Dion, Dionys, Dionysios, Diwis, Donisi, Donisl,

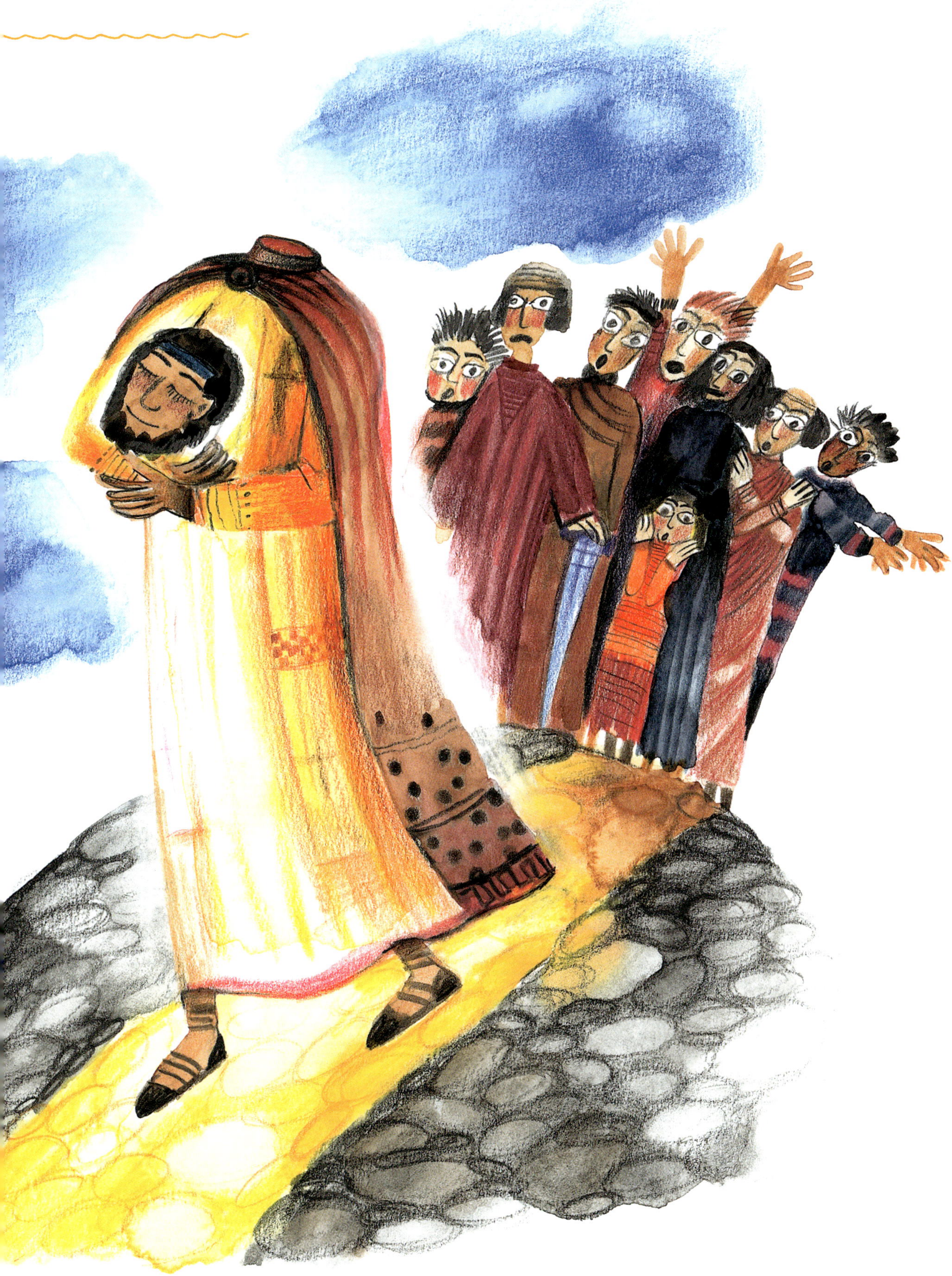

TERESA OF AVILA

15 OCTOBER

Teresa was a bright child and loved reading. Her favourite book was one about the saints. She loved God and decided that like some of the saints in her book, she would like to become a martyr and die for her faith. She imagined going to the Moors, who were at that time the enemy of the Christians, and telling them of her belief in Christ. Once they knew that she would never reject Christianity, she felt sure they would kill her. She would then go straight to heaven as a martyr. This thought remained with her always.

She was born in 1515 in Avila in Spain. At the age of twenty she joined a Carmelite convent as a religious sister. When she saw how the other sisters ignored the convent rules, she was very unhappy. They seemed to do just what they wanted. Many sat around all day chatting, and some even had their own servants.

Again and again Teresa heard the voice of God, telling her he was close to her, and consoling her in her troubles. Once, when she became very sick she felt God was trying to tell her something special. When she recovered and gradually became stronger, she decided that God wanted something else from her. She told others and began to inspire many in the order to change their lives.

She established a new religious order called the Discalced Carmelite Nuns (discalced, barefoot or wearing only sandals). More and more women joined her and new convents were built and the order flourished. Later, St John of the Cross, assisted her in founding a similar order for men. Teresa died on 4th October 1582, and in 1970, almost four hundred years after her death she was given the honorary title of Doctor of the Church.

Theresa was outspoken and encouraged others to change their lives. Who inspires you to lead a better life?

Resa, Resi, Resia, Teresa, Terezie, Terka, Terri, Terry, Tess, Tessa, Thea, Therese, Thérèse, Theresina, Thersa, Thery, Thesi, Tracy

LUKE

18 OCTOBER

Luke lived at the same time as Jesus, but they never met. Nevertheless, Luke knew a great deal about Jesus from the apostle Paul, who was his friend. Paul told him about the teachings of Jesus in such great detail, that he too was able to spread the message of Jesus in many countries. Because of this, he can be considered to be an apostle. Luke also learned about Jesus from Mary, the mother of Jesus.

He was so moved by all that he heard about Jesus, he wanted to write it down. He wanted people to know, the love and compassion Jesus had for the sick, the poor and the needy, and his love and pity for sinners. He wanted to keep the memory of Jesus alive, and so he wrote what we now know as Luke's Gospel. A person who writes a Gospel is called an evangelist. The symbol for Luke is the winged ox. He later wrote a book called 'The Acts of the Apostles'.

It is thought that Luke probably came from Antioch in Syria, where he was born several years before the birth of Jesus. He was a famous doctor who was well known for his great knowledge. By the year 50 AD he had met Paul. They became good friends, and since Luke was not then a Christian, Paul baptised him. He then accompanied Paul on his missionary journeys. After the death of Paul, Luke probably went to Greece where he worked as a bishop until his death.

Because Luke wrote so lovingly about Mary in his Gospel, the legend grew that he had also 'painted' a beautiful picture of Mary. There are some very old pictures of Mary, which people claim were painted by Luke.

> Luke was a man who cared for the poor and sick with great gentleness. Do you find gentleness with others easy or difficult?

Laux, Luc, Luca, Lucano, Lucas, Lucca, Lukarz, Lukasz, Lukian, Lutz

111

Ursula

21 October

If you look closely at the municipal coat of arms of the city of Cologne in Germany, you will see three crowns in gold and eleven black flames. The crowns represent the three wise men whose shrine is in the cathedral. The eleven flames represent Ursula and her ten companions. There are many different legends about the life of Ursula. Within these legends there is always a grain of truth.

It is thought that Ursula was the daughter of a British king and a devout Christian. Aetherius, the son of a pagan king wanted to marry her, but Ursula had always wanted to devote her life to Christ. She had no wish to marry anyone. However, she knew that if she rejected him there would be war between the two kingdoms. Reluctantly she promised to marry him. She asked if he would delay the marriage for three years, so that she could make a pilgrimage to Rome. Aetherius readily agreed. He also promised that on her return he would become a Christian.

She was given as companions for the journey, ten young women of noble birth. They set out by ship for Rome and upon their arrival they were received by the pope. The return journey was beset by problems. There was a terrific storm and the ship got into difficulties. Ursula and her friends were put ashore at Cologne, a city on the river Rhine.

The Huns were besieging the city of Cologne at that time. They killed Ursula's companions, but they spared Ursula. The leader of the invaders admired Ursula's beauty and wanted to marry her. Ursula refused and he immediately turned on her and killed her with an arrow.

Ursula and her friends met with storms and cruelty on their journey. In what way can you show courage when faced with difficulties in life's journey?

Orseli, Orsina, Orsola, Orsolina, Orsolya, Ulla, Ulli, Ursa, Urschel, Ursel, Ursetta, Ursina, Ursina, Ursl, Ursola, Ursule, Ursulina, Uschi

Simon

28 OCTOBER

Simon the Zealot was a follower of Jesus and was one of the twelve apostles. Unlike the apostle Simon, who later became Peter, Simon the Zealot was very quiet. Little has been written about him in the Gospels, but Jesus must have been impressed by the modesty of this unassuming disciple. He knew that these are often the very people who are especially loyal and reliable. No one knows the time and circumstances of Simon's call by Jesus to join the apostles. Possibly he was a relative of another apostle who had told him about Jesus.

Simon had been a follower of those who were prepared to fight for the freedom of the Jewish people, suffering at that time under the Roman reign of terror. That was why he had the name 'Zealot'. The zealots were the men who organised resistance groups among the people, against the Romans. The Romans had seized power and were demanding that the people pay heavy taxes to the Roman emperor. The men Simon associated with wanted to expel the Romans by force.

They risked their lives by staging demonstrations and organising raids against them. Because the zealots fought so fearlessly for the freedom of their country they were admired by many of the people.

However, once Simon answered the call of Jesus to become an apostle, he became quite a different person. Jesus had no time for violence. He knew that you should not fight violence with further violence. After the death of Jesus it is said that Simon went to Persia and preached the good news of Jesus there. Eventually he was martyred for his beliefs. Images often show him carrying a saw, indicating the way he died. Because of this symbol, Simon is regarded as the patron of lumberjacks and forest workers.

> Simon tried to change the world without violence after he met Jesus. How can we encourage people to use peaceful means to change society?

Semjon, Siem, Sim, Sima, Simeon, Simeone, Simmel, Simmie, Simone, Syma

4 NOVEMBER

CHARLES BORROMEO

As a bishop, he dedicated himself totally to the care of his diocese and its people. He realised that a good diocese needed good priests, so he set about looking after them. He also encouraged the priests, in their turn, to look after their parishioners. He was not afraid to correct those who had jobs in the Church, but were not diligent in their work.

He built seminaries, where new priests could be trained for the priesthood. He also supported the mission work of the religious orders in his diocese. In this way he brought many people back to the practice of their faith. It was the example of his own life which impressed people. He never asked his priests to do anything he wasn't prepared to do himself. The people loved and admired him for it.

Charles Borromeo was born in 1538 into one of the most influential families in Italy. But of all the great people in the family he was probably the most outstanding. He was born in a town by the name of Arona, situated on the southern shore of Lake Maggiore in Northern Italy.

Charles began his studies at the university of Milan and was an exceptional student. He was given great responsibility in the Church even before he was ordained. Because of his ability and wealthy connections, he could have made a career in managing the Church's property. He decided however he would like to become a priest. Very soon he was consecrated as Bishop of Milan.

Day and night, Charles showed personal concern for the sick and the dying, especially during the long months of the plague, when many thousands of people in Milan died. Totally exhausted by the work, he often neglected his own health, sometimes eating just bread and water. This dedication to his people totally weakened him and Charles Borromeo died at the age of forty-six on 3rd November 1584.

Charles helped the poor and challenged others to be more responsible. How can you be more honest, generous and helpful?

Carel, Carl, Carlo, Carlos, Charlie, Karel, Károly

LEONARD

6 NOVEMBER

Leonard was born into a wealthy family and lived in the north of France. He became a priest and people were so impressed by the good he did that he was soon nominated as bishop. Although he realised that it was a great honour to be a bishop, Leonard preferred to work amongst the people as an ordinary priest. He wanted to devote his energy working for those who had been released from prison. He wanted to find a way to help them to make a new life for themselves. This was constantly on his mind. Eventually he left the town and escaped into the forest to live in solitude and prayer.

Soon people started to come to him to ask for help. Amongst his many skills he was also able to cure sick animals. He was particularly skilled at curing sick horses. As his reputation grew, more and more people brought their animals to him.

One day, it happened that the queen, who was expecting a baby, was riding through the forest. As she passed the cottage, where Leonard lived, her labour pains started. Leonard looked after her until her child was born.

The king was so grateful to him he said that Leonard could have anything he wished. Leonard asked for as much of the forest as a donkey could walk through in one night. His strange wish was granted, and Leonard made the land into a refuge for released prisoners.

Later a famous monastery was built on the ground near Limoges and it was named the monastery of St Léonard. Leonard lived to be an old man and died on 6th November in the year 559.

It not surprising that, to this day, Leonard is considered the patron saint of horses and livestock.

Leonard realised that once prisoners were released they needed help to change their ways. How could you help someone to make better choices?

Lehnhard, Len, Lenard, Lenardo, Lenhard, Lennart, Lenz, Leo, Leon, Leonardo, Leonz, Lionardo

11 NOVEMBER

MARTIN

The story of how Martin divided his cloak, and gave half of it to a poor man, has become the symbol of concern for the needy throughout the ages. It is a story of great generosity and compassion. There are still many poor people in the world who need our help. The example set by Martin is still relevant today. A great deal of what we know about Martin is from the writings of a monk called Sulpicius Severus, who knew and respected him.

Martin was born in the year 317 in Pannonia, which today is part of Hungary. Martin's parents didn't believe in Jesus Christ and educated their son in pagan ways. Martin spent most of his childhood in Northern Italy and met many Christians. They always impressed him and when a local priest told him about Jesus, Martin decided he wanted to be baptised. Furthermore, he wanted to become a monk. Martin's father was a high-ranking Roman soldier and decided Martin would follow him, into a career in the army. This was not what Martin wanted, but he respected his father's decision and agreed to become a soldier. However, in his heart, he still kept alive the dream of being baptised a Christian.

As a soldier, Martin was sent to Amiens in France. Unlike many of the other soldiers, Martin was a very quiet person. He was also brave and courageous. His superiors recognised his strength of character by giving him promotion in the army and a servant to wait on him. From the beginning Martin treated the servant with kindness and generosity. This annoyed his fellow soldiers. It was not the custom to treat servants in this way and they mocked Martin mercilessly.

> Martin was not afraid to do what was right even though others teased him. How do you stand up for what is right when others tease you?

Maarten, Maartinus, Marcin, Mart, Märte, Marten, Marti, Märti, Martien, Martijn, Martino, Martinus, Martl, Mertel, Merten, Mertin, Mirtel, Morten

One cold winter's day as Martin rode through the city gate, he saw a poor beggar huddled on the ground. He was wearing hardly any clothes and was shivering. As people passed by they ignored him. Martin couldn't understand their lack of feeling for the man. He immediately took his sword and cut his own cloak in two and gave half to the beggar. That night, in a dream, Martin saw Jesus Christ holding out a piece of the cloak he had given away. He heard Jesus say, "Martin, who is not yet baptised, covered me with this cloak."

Martin was so moved he knew what he must do. He left the army and was baptised. He became a recluse on an island near Milan. There, he founded a monastery called Ligug. When the Bishop of Tours in France died, the townspeople tricked Martin into visiting the town so that they could make him bishop. When Martin agreed, he insisted that he lived in a monastery as a monk and not in the bishop's palace.

During his years as bishop Martin travelled from house to house, telling people about God. Many came to love and know Jesus through the kindness of Martin. He lived to be over eighty years old and died in the year 397 AD. The news of his death spread like wildfire. From all the surrounding areas people streamed to his funeral in Tours. Thousands of monks joined the funeral procession. He was buried in the Cemetery of the Poor in Tours.

19 NOVEMBER

ELIZABETH

Elizabeth was a Hungarian princess who, as a child, captured everyone with her beautiful smile. As was often the case with aristocratic families in the Middle Ages, she was forced by her parents to marry when she was very young. Fortunately for Elisabeth, the husband chosen for her was a man she really loved, a count by the name of Louis of Thuringia. It was a happy marriage. Louis lived with his bride in the famous castle of Wartburg. In time Elizabeth and Louis were blessed with three children Herman, Sophie and Gertrude.

However, when Elizabeth looked around Wartburg, what she saw made her very sad. The ordinary people lived in dire poverty with hardly anything to eat. Many were homeless and were dying of diseases because they could not afford to pay for doctors or hospitals. Much of their poverty was the result of the heavy taxes they had to pay to their rulers who live in palaces.

# of Hungary

The nobility lived in splendour and luxury on the money they collected from the poor.

Elizabeth was desperately upset by this situation. She decided to change her lifestyle radically. She changed from the rich clothes of the nobility into the simple garments of ordinary people. Instead of eating her food from golden plates, she ate rough bread with her maids in the kitchen. From the castle granaries, she gave away grain to the poor and nursed the sick people she found on the streets. Elizabeth wanted to be like Jesus Christ. She wanted to give and to share, to help everyone, just as Jesus had done. She was ready to suffer for this way of life, to endure scorn and mockery and even to die.

Louis, her husband, supported his beloved wife as well as he could, despite the many reproaches he had to put up with from the rest of the family. Her wealthy relatives made life very difficult for Elizabeth. Louis's family tormented and derided her. However no matter what they said, nothing ever discouraged her. Every day she went out from the castle in search of those who were poor or suffering. One day she happened to meet Henry, her brother-in-law. He asked her what she was carrying in her basket. It was bread that Elizabeth was taking to feed some lepers. However as Henry pulled the cloth off the basket, beautiful red roses lay there.

Elizabeth smiled and thanked God for the miracle. Henry was highly embarrassed by the incident.

Then things seemed to go desperately wrong for the family. Her husband, Louis, became sick and died. The young Elizabeth and her children were immediately thrown out of their home in the castle of Wartburg. Although she had many proposals of marriage from wealthy men, the young widow refused to remarry. Louis's family disowned her and left her without any money. Her children were taken from her and placed in an orphanage. This treatment destroyed Elisabeth. How could she live without her children and without caring for the poor? Her whole life had been devoted to them. She weakened very rapidly and on 19th November 1231 she died. Today Elizabeth is still regarded as a wonderful example of charity and concern for the poor.

Elizabeth shared her riches with others. Do you find it easy to share what you have with others?

Alice, Alison, Babette, Bella, Beth, Betina, Betti, Bettina, Betty, Élice, Elis, Elisa, Elisabetha, Elisabetta, Ella, Elli, Ellis, Elly, Elsa, Elsbeth, Isabel, Isabella, Lisa, Lisbeth, Lise, Liz, Liza, Sisi, Sissi, Sissy

22 NOVEMBER

CECILIA

The story of Cecilia is outstanding in Christian tradition. Cecilia was born in Rome at the beginning of the third century. It was a time when Christians were suffering great persecutions throughout the Roman Empire. Many were killed for their belief in Jesus Christ. When she was very young, Cecilia decided she would never marry. She wanted to devote her life to Jesus.

She grew into a beautiful young woman. At that time, when young women reached a certain age they were expected to marry. They could not choose to live on their own. Cecilia's parents forced her into marriage with a young man named Valerian, who was not a Christian. Cecilia was very upset, but trusted in Jesus to guide her to do what was right.

On the day of their wedding, Cecilia told Valerian the marriage could not take place. She told him of her vow never to marry, but to live only for Jesus Christ. Valerian, who loved Cecilia very much, asked her what he should do. She suggested that he should become a Christian and be baptised. On his way back from the celebration of his baptism, he saw Cecilia praying, and an angel was by her with flaming wings, holding two crowns of roses and lilies, which were placed on their heads.

From that moment on, Valerian worked unremittingly with Cecilia for the spread of the Christian faith. Together they comforted Christians who were imprisoned, and arranged the funerals of those who were martyred. The martyrs were the Christians who were put to death for their faith.

One day, those who hated the Christians killed Valerian. With great courage Cecilia publicly professed that she too was a Christian. The persecutors decided that she should die too and she was thrown into a bath of boiling water. Cecilia came out of it without a mark on her. She was totally unscathed. Terrified by this miracle, they decided to cut off her head. Three times the executioner struck Cecilia with his sword. Three times she survived. After three days of agony, she died on 22nd November in the year 230 AD. Cecilia was thirty years old.

Cecilia and Valerian worked together to share God's message. How could you spread God's message to those you meet in your daily life?

Cécile, Cecily, Sheila, Sheilah, Sheela, Sheelah, Shelah, Selia, Sheilagh.

ANDREW

30 NOVEMBER

Andrew was a fisherman from Palestine. He looked forward to meeting the Messiah, the Redeemer. However, he was worried that he would not recognize him. Andrew had heard that John, known as 'the Baptist', had announced that the Messiah was coming soon. Andrew thought it would be a good idea to stay close to John, in the hope of being there when the Messiah came.

The plan worked well. One day, John the Baptist pointed to a man and said to Andrew and his friend John,
"This is the lamb of God."
The man was Jesus. Andrew was very excited and, together with John, he ran up to Jesus. Jesus turned around and asked them what they wanted. Andrew was embarrassed. He didn't know what to say. So he enquired,
"Master, where do you live?"
Jesus smiled and greeted them. When Andrew arrived home that evening, he excitedly told his brother Simon,
"We've found the Messiah."

Some time later, Andrew and Simon were fishing in Lake Galilee. Jesus came up to them and said,
"Follow me, I will make you into fishers of men."
They were not sure what he meant, but they followed him. Andrew and Simon became the first two apostles of Jesus. Soon, they began to understand what Jesus meant by 'fishers of men'. In time they would go out and tell people about the teachings of Jesus and they would come to know and love him.

Throughout his time with Jesus, Andrew remained in the background. Jesus knew that, if he needed his help, he was there. After the death and resurrection of Jesus, Andrew visited many different countries, telling people about Jesus and preaching the good news.

It is believed that he was killed for his faith about the year 60 AD. He was nailed to a cross in the shape of the letter X. This type of cross is known as the Saint Andrew Cross. Saint Andrew is now revered as the patron saint of Scotland.

Andrew the apostle was quietly dependable. In what way can your friends depend on you?

Anders, Andi, Andor, André, Andrea, Andrei, Andrej, Andres, Andries, Andy

3 DECEMBER

FRANCIS XAVIER

Francis Xavier is one of the greatest examples of what it means to be a missionary. He was born in the village of Xavier, near Pamplona in the Basque area of Spain on 7th April 1506. He went to Paris to study, where he lived a wild life. A friend, by the name of Ignatius of Loyola, constantly had to lend him money.

One day, he discovered that Ignatius was establishing a religious order called 'The Company of Jesus', now known as the Jesuits. Francis was so impressed by his friend's commitment, and so disillusioned by the kind of empty life he was living, he decided to join the order and become a priest.

The pope sent Francis Xavier to India, to work as a missionary. The journey to India was a voyage of thirteen months. When he arrived there he immediately began to study the local language and to understand the customs of the people. He lived with them and cared for them. Francis was convinced that a missionary could only be successful if he respected the local customs. He did not believe in just baptising people, he wanted to win the hearts of the people. He wanted to help them to respect him and so bring them to understand the teachings of Jesus Christ.

Soon, thousands came to Francis to hear about Jesus and to be baptised. Again and again he prolonged his mission trips. In 1549 he landed in Japan. The entire first year was devoted to learning the Japanese language. During his years on the missions Francis wrote more than 1000 letters about his work. His letters were so inspirational that many young people, all over the world, followed his example and became missionaries. After many mission journeys, Francis was completely exhausted. This great missionary died on 3rd December 1552, when he was forty-six years old.

? Francis spent time getting to know and understand people before he began his work. How could this approach be useful in today's troubled world?

Ferenc, Franc, Francesco, Francisco, Francisk, Francisque, Franciszek, Franco, Francois, Franek, Frank, Franjo, Frans, Frantz, Javier, Saverio, Savy, Vere, Xabier, Xaverius, Xavery, Xavier, Zaverio

BARBARA

4 DECEMBER

According to legend, Barbara was the extremely beautiful daughter of a wealthy heathen named Dioscorus, who lived near Nicomedia in Asia Minor. Because of her great beauty, her father was worried that she would be demanded in marriage and taken away from him, so he jealously shut her up in a tower to protect her from the outside world.

Barbara had heard of the teachings of Jesus Christ, and, while her father was not with her, she spent much of her time deep in thought. From her tower she looked out of the windows and marvelled at the animals, the people, and the beautiful countryside. She decided that all these must be part of a master plan, and that the idols of wood and stone worshipped by her parents must be condemned as false. Gradually she came to accept the Christian faith.

As her belief became stronger, she directed that the builders re-design the tower, adding another window so that the three windows might symbolize the Holy Trinity, God the Father, God the Son and God the Holy Spirit. When her father returned, he was angry at the changes. He was even more furious when Barbara told him that she was a Christian.

He dragged her before the prefect of the province, who decreed that she be tortured and put to death by beheading.

Her father Diocorus carried out the death sentence. As she was dying beautiful flowers appeared in he room. On his way home Diocorus was struck by lightening and died.

Barbara lived at the beginning of the fourth century. The legend of the lightning bolt, which struck down her killer, caused her to be regarded as the patron saint of those in danger from thunderstorms, fires and sudden death. When gunpowder was brought to the Western world, many of the early guns often blew up instead of firing. Saint Barbara was invoked for aid against accidents resulting from explosions. She was therefore also known as the patron saint of artillery men.

> Barbara was full of wonder at the beauty of God's creation. How is that beauty being spoiled today?

Babette, Babro, Babs, Balba, Barbe, Barberina, Barbi, Barbli, Barbra, Barbro, Basia

6 DECEMBER

NICHOLAS

Nicholas, better known as Santa Claus, is one of the most popular saints for children in many parts of Europe. He is often portrayed as a man in a red coat with a white beard. All the stories about Nicholas, tell us that as bishop of Myra, he was highly respected. He was renowned far and wide for his kindness. His fellow bishops had great admiration for their colleague Nicholas; he had all the qualities one would expect to find in a bishop.

He was born in the year 270 AD in a small port called Patara. This was in a country, which is now known as Turkey. He was ordained priest by his uncle who was a bishop. His parents died at quite an early age leaving their wealth to Nicholas. He did not want riches and gave all of his inheritance away to the poor.

One day, Nicholas got up early to travel to a place called Myra, about fifty miles away. He stopped at the main church in the city to say his morning prayers. When he arrived there, he was surprised to find so many people already in the church. When they saw him, they immediately cried out that they wanted him to be their bishop. The people had been without a bishop for some months.

They had agreed among themselves, that whatever priest came into the church first that morning, he would become their new bishop. In this way Nicholas was chosen as the new bishop of Myra.

This was not a time of peace for those who believed in Jesus. The Roman Emperor was still persecuting Christians. Many were being thrown into prison for practising their faith. Nicholas stood by his fellow Christians and was a great source of comfort for them in their suffering. However, this made the Romans very angry. One day, Nicholas himself was thrown into prison and had to suffer many miseries. All of this he endured without complaining. Impressed by his bravery, the Romans set him free. The whole city came to the prison rejoicing at his freedom.

There are so many stories about the generosity of Nicholas, and the way he cared for his people. Whenever they were in need, they came to him. Once he saved three innocent men who had been sentenced to death. Another time, he came to the help of a poor family that could not care for their three daughters and were considering selling them off into slavery. At night, he crept quietly up to their cottage and threw three bags of gold coins through the window. This enabled the girls to remain at home to care for their sick parents.

> Nicholas had the ability to recognise people's needs and find ways to help them. How could you more quickly understand the needs of those around you?

Claas, Claes, Colin, Klas, Klaus, Mikola, Mikolaj, Nick, Nicky, Niclaus, Nico, Nicol, Nicolaas, Nicolas, Nicolau, Nicole, Nicolo, Niels, Nikita, Nikkel, Niklas, Niklaus, Niko, Nikol, Nikolaas, Nikolai, Nikolaos, Nikolas

It is said that when the kindly Nicholas died in the year 350 AD, almost everyone in his diocese cried. They all agreed that God could not have had a better representative on earth than Nicholas.

The people loved him so much that they were constantly putting roses on his grave.

Devotion to Saint Nicholas spread to many countries, particularly in Greece and Russia. There are quite a few traditions associated with Saint Nicholas. In many parts of Europe he is Santa Claus, who brings sweets and presents to children on the eve of December 6th, the feast day of St Nicholas, or on December 24th, Christmas Eve. Legend has it, that for many years after his death, Nicholas was seen walking through the snow at Christmas in his old city of Myra. He was wrapped up well, so that no one recognized him. It has been said that he was seen going to the cottages of the poor and laying golden apples at their door. Perhaps this story was invented because people simply wanted to keep the memory of Nicholas alive. We will never know.

LUCY

13 DECEMBER

The name Lucy means 'light'. When we say a thing is 'lucid' we mean it is clear or radiant. When parents give their daughter this name at baptism, they are hoping that their child will illuminate their lives.

Lucy was a Christian, who lived at the beginning of the fourth century. Her home town was Syracuse, on the Italian island of Sicily. It was the dearest wish of her sick mother that Lucy be married. But Lucy wanted to dedicate her life to Jesus, rather than marry. However, she kept these thoughts to herself, she didn't want to upset her mother.

One day, Lucy suggested that they make a pilgrimage to the tomb of Saint Agatha to pray for her mother's healing. Following the visit, a wonderful miracle happened, her mother was cured, and she allowed Lucy to put aside all thoughts of marriage. Lucy was overjoyed. Now, she could devote her life to Jesus.

Her joy soon turned to sadness. The man Lucy's mother had already chosen as her bridegroom, was so upset by the cancellation of the wedding, he took her to court. Lucy was not afraid of the judge. She courageously stood in front of him, and declared loudly that she loved only Jesus. She knew that acknowledging her belief in Christ could result in her death. Later she was thrown onto an ox cart to be taken to her execution. But the ox could not move the cart. The judge angrily ordered that Lucy should be immersed in boiling oil, but she remained uninjured. He was so frightened by what had happened, he gave a final command and Lucy was killed by the sword.

To this day there is the custom in Sweden, for the eldest girl in the family to go round the house on Saint Lucy's feast day, with a wreath of burning candles, early in the morning. She awakens the rest of the family and tells them that soon they will be celebrating the birth of Jesus, the light of the world.

Lucy knew that the coming of Jesus brought light to the world. In what way does someone bring light into your life?

Lucetta, Luci, Luciana, Luciana, Lucie, Lucienne, Lucilla, Lucille, Lucina, Lucin Lukesa, Lusinde, Luz, Luzia, Luziane

STEPHEN

26 DECEMBER

Stephen was prepared to die rather than give up his belief in Christ. He is considered to be the first martyr in the history of the Christian Church.

After the death of Jesus in Jerusalem, the apostles chose seven men as deacons, who would devote their lives to caring for the poor. One of these men was Stephen. He soon attracted much attention. He announced the Gospel so powerfully that the people were fascinated by him. Crowds came to see him and listened as he spread the good news about Jesus. They witnessed his many miracles and admired him more and more. As his enemies watched, they became aware of how popular he had become. They became envious of him and plotted to get rid of him.

They invented false charges against Stephen and he was dragged before the court. They said they had heard him speak words of blasphemy against Moses and God. This charge angered the rowdy mob. As Stephen knelt down to pray, he was pelted with heavy stones. This continued until he was dead. Even as he was dying, Stephen shamed his enemies. He looked up to heaven and prayed,
"Lord, do not hold this sin against them."
He had already forgiven his murderers. Now he was asking God to forgive them as well.

When we think of Stephen, we are reminded of the strength required to show forgiveness. It may seem surprising that in our Church calendar while on the 25th December we cheerfully celebrate the birth of Jesus and only one day later on the 26th December, we celebrate the feast of Stephen, who died for his belief in Jesus Christ.

> Stephen trusted the words of Jesus that we should forgive those who hurt us. Why do we sometimes find it difficult to forgive those who are unkind to us?

Estéban, Estévan, Estienne, Étienne, István, Sczepan, Stefan, Stefano, Steffen, Stepan, Stéphane, Stephanos, Stephanus, Stepka, Stepko, Steve, Steven, Stevie

27 DECEMBER
JOHN, Apostle and Evangelist

John taught us an important lesson. He said, "If somebody says that he loves God but hates his brother, then he is a liar."
These words remind us that the best way to judge the love we have for God, is to look at the way we treat each other.

Jesus called John and his older brother James, 'The Sons of Thunder'. John was a man who always spoke his mind. Jesus valued the honesty of John, the youngest of the apostles. He considered John as a special friend. This is why John was often referred to as the 'Favourite Disciple'.

John believed in Jesus and stood by him till the end. He was the only apostle to stand fearlessly at the foot of the cross, to which the Romans had crucified the Son of God. The other apostles were frightened and had run away. It became clear how much Jesus loved John when he asked him to take care of his mother Mary after his death. He told him,
"Son, this is your mother."
He wanted John to look after her, as if she were his own mother.

After the death of Jesus, John was one of the most important apostles in Jerusalem. He took upon himself the responsibility of preaching the Gospel, and because of this he was arrested three times. Later, he left Jerusalem in order to carry the message of Jesus to other countries. He went to the city of Ephesus, which is in present day Turkey. There, he had great success and established seven Christian communities.

During those years, he wrote his famous Book of Revelations. He also wrote three important letters and his Gospel. His symbol is that of the eagle. It is said that John lived to a very great age and died in Ephesus.

John showed that to love God we must first love each other. How can we make sure we treat others as we wish to be treated ourselves?

Eoin, Evan, Gianni, Giovanni, Hans, Hanke, Hanko, Hannemann, Hannes, Hans, Iaian, Ian, Ivan, Iven, Iwan, Jack, Jan, Jannis, Jean, Johann, Juan, Nino, Seain, Sean, Shane, Shawn, Zane

David

29 DECEMBER

Many people believe that if they are big and strong, they will have power; it will bring them success. However, the story of David shows us that success does not come from might but from a belief in yourself.

David was a young boy who lived before the time of Christ. He was just a poor shepherd keeping watch over the sheep, which belonged to his family. War had broken out between the Philistines and the Israelites, and David was an Israelite. Three of his brothers went to fight against the Philistines and their father Jesse constantly worried about them. He heard that in the Philistine army there was a giant of a man with immense strength. Finally Jesse could endure the worry no longer and he sent David into the war camp to make sure his brothers were safe.

When David arrived he couldn't believe his eyes. There, on the hill, where the Philistines had their camp, stood a giant with a long spear. He was called Goliath. Again and again, the giant yelled out for everyone to hear. He challenged any man to fight him. Everyone was terrified; they could not imagine anyone being brave enough to stand up to Goliath. No Israelite dared consider it. It would take more than one man to defeat the giant.

David knew that he did not have the strength to defeat Goliath, but thought perhaps he could beat the giant by using his brain. With great confidence he shouted out to the giant, "Come on, I'm the man to fight with you!" Goliath stamped his feet and, as he did, the earth shook. David was not intimidated. With great courage he called back,

"God stands on our side. He will defeat you."

Secretly, David had packed five flat stones and a slingshot. By now the giant was getting quite angry. David stretched the sling tight and released a stone; the stone struck Goliath right between the eyes. As if struck by an axe Goliath fell to the ground. David's stone had killed him.

David's confidence in accepting the challenge and his bravery in facing him had beaten the giant. The Israelites rejoiced, with the death of Goliath, they had won the war. Years later, David became king of the Israelites. His people never forgot how, by his courage he had rescued them.

> David put his trust and God and believed in himself. In what way can you develop a belief in your own abilities?

Dabi, Dave, Davidde, Davide, Davis, Davy, Daw, Dawes, Taffy

31 DECEMBER

SYLVESTER

New Year's Eve is usually a time of celebration. On 31st December everyone is saying goodbye to the old year and looking forward to a new year and a new beginning. It is the custom for everyone to wish each other many blessings for the coming year. However, hardly anyone thinks of the saint whose feast is celebrated on 31st December.

Sylvester was pope at an important time in the Church. It was the time when the persecution of the Christians by the Romans was over and they could live in peace. Emperor Constantine brought about this change. He introduced a law in the year 313 AD which protected the Christians. He was supported by his mother Helena.

A new pope had to be chosen and Constantine wanted Sylvester to be the head of the Church. Sylvester had a reputation of being both intelligent and kind. But Sylvester was still in hiding because he didn't know that the Christians were no longer persecuted. The emperor finally found him in a mountain cave. On New Year's Eve he was solemnly escorted to Rome and he was consecrated as Pope Sylvester I.

Sylvester and Constantine worked well together. With the support of the Emperor, Sylvester brought Christianity to the empire. In Rome he built great churches. The most important of these being St Peter's Basilica on the site where Peter the apostle was killed. One of the most important Church Meetings, the famous Council of Nicea, took place during Sylvester's term of office.

Despite his successes, Sylvester always remained a very humble person. Often, he retreated into the mountains in order to pray. After 21 years as pope, Sylvester died on the 31st December in the year 335 AD.

Sylvester achieved great things in his life but remained humble. Do you know someone who has remained humble although they have achieved great success in their life?

Fester, Silvest, Silvestre, Silvestro, Sly, Süster, Sylvester, Sylvestre, Syste, Syster, Vester

Saints and Special People in Alphabetical Order

A

Adalbert of Prague 23 April p 35
Adrian 8 September
Aedh MacBricc 10 November
Agatha 5 February
Agnes 21 January p 13
Agnes of Assisi 16 November
Agnes of Bayern 11 November
Agnes of Böhmen 2 March
Aidan of Lindisfarne 31 August
Alban 20 June
Albert the Great 15 November
Alexander I 3 May p 41
Alexander of Rome 10 July
Alexis 17 July
Aloysius Gonzaga 21 June
Alphonsus Liguori 1 August
Ambrose Barlow 10 September
Ambrose of Milan 7 December
Andrew Avellino 10 November
Andrew Corsini 6 January
Andrew Dung-Lac and Companions 24 November
Andrew Kim and Companions 20 September
Andrew the Apostle 30 November p 121
Angela Merici 27 January p 15
Angela of Foligno 4 January
Anne Line 30 August
Anne Mother of Mary 26 July p 74
Anselm of Canterbury 21 April
Ansgar 3 February
Anthony Claret 24 October
Anthony of Padua 13 June p 54
Anthony the Great 17 January
Anthony Zaccaria 5 July
Arnold 8 July
Arnold Janssen 15 January
Athanasius 2 May
Augustine 28 August p 87
Augustine of Canterbury 27 May
Augustine Zhao Rong 9 July

B

Balthasar 6 January p 10
Barbara 4 December p 123
Barnabas 11 June
Bartholomew 24 August p 85
Basil the Great 2 January
Benedict Biscop 12 January
Benedict of Nursia 11 July p 62
Benedict-Joseph Labré 16 April
Benjamin 31 March p 32
Bernadette Soubirous 16 April p 33
Bernard of Aosta 15 June
Bernard of Clairvaux 20 August p 84
Bernardine of Siena 20 May
Bertha May 15
Blaise 3 February p 18
Bonaventura 15 July
Boniface 5 June p 52
Boniface of Canterbury 14 July
Boniface of Tarsos 14 May
Brendan May 16
Bridget of Ireland 1 February
Bridget of Sweden 23 July p 70
Brogan September 17
Bruno 6 October

C

Casimir 4 March p 25
Casper 6 January p 10
Catherine of Siena 29 April p 38
Cecilia 22 November p 120
Charles Borromeo 4 November p 114
Charles Lwanga and Companions 3 June
Christina of Bolsena 24 July p 72
Christopher 24 July p 71
Clare of Assisi 11 August p 80
Conrad 21 April p 34
Cosmas 26 September p 96
Cunegundes 13 July p 64
Cyril 14 February p 22

D

Damian 26 September p 96
Damien of Molokai April 15
Daniel 21 July p 66
David 29 December p 129
David of Wales 1 March

Denis of Paris 9 October p 108
Dermot 10 January
Dismas 25 March
Dominic 8 August p 78
Dominic Barberi 26 August
Dominic Savio 6 May
Donald 15 July
Dorothy 6 February p 20
Dorothy of Montau 25 June
Dunstan 19 May
Dyfan 26 May
Dymphna 15 May

E

Edith Stein 9 August
Edmund Arrowsmith 1 September
Edmund Campion 1 December
Edmund Ignatius Rice 5 May
Edward the Confessor 13 October
Edwin 12 October
Elizabeth Ann Seton 4 January
Elizabeth Mother of John 5 November
Elizabeth of Hungary 19 November p 118
Elizabeth of Portugal 4 July
Ephrem June 9
Eric of Sweden 10 July
Ethelbert May 20
Etheldreda 23 June

F

Fabian 20 January
Faustina Kowalska 5 October p 106
Felicity 7 March
Felix of Cantalice 18 May p 46
Felix of Dunwich 8 March
Felix of Nola 14 January
Felix of Valois 20 November
Finbar 25 September
Finian 10 September
Fintan 3 January
Florian 4 May p 42
Frances of Chantal 12 December
Frances of Rome 9 March p 27
Francesca Cabrini 13 November

Francis de Borja 1 October
Francis de Sales 24 January
Francis of Assisi 4 October p 104
Francis of Paola 2 April
Francis Xavier 3 December p 122
Frederick of Utrecht 18 July

G

Gabriel Archangel 29 September p 101
Genevieve 3 January
George 23 April p 36
George Haydock 10 February
Gerard Majella 16 October
Gertrude 17 March
Gilbert of Sempringham 16 February
Giles 1 September
Gladys 29 March
Gregory of Nazianzen 2 January
Gregory the Great 3 September
Gwen 18 October

H

Harold March 25
Hedwig of Silesia 16 October
Helena Empress 18 August
Henry King 13 July p 64
Henry of Finland 19 January
Henry Suso 23 January
Hilary of Poitiers 13 January
Hilda 17 November
Hildegard of Bingen 17 September p 91
Hubert of Maastricht 3 November
Hugh of Lincoln 17 November
Hugo of Grenoble 1 April

I

Ignatius of Antioch 17 October
Ignatius of Loyola 31 July p 76
Irenaeus 28 June
Isaac Jogues & Companions 19 October
Isidore of Seville 4 April
Ita January 15

J

James the Great 25 July p 73
James the Less 3 May p 40
Jerome 30 September
Joachim Father of Mary 26 July p 74
Joachim of Fiore 30 March
Joachim Piccolomini 16 April
Joan of Arc 30 May p 50
Joan of Lestonnac 2 February
Joan of Portugal 12 May
Joan of Valois 4 February
John Apostle and Evangelist 27 December p 128
John Baptist de la Salle 7 April
John Berchmans 13 August
John Bosco 31 January p 16
John Boste 24 July
John Chrysostom 13 September
John Damascene 4 December
John de Brebeuf 19 October
John Duns Scotus 8 November
John Houghton 4 May
John Nepomucene 16 May p 44
John Neumann 5 January
John of Beverly 7 May
John of Capistrano 23 October
John of God 8 March p 26
John of the Cross 14 December
John Ogilvie 10 March
John Payne 4 May
John Plessington 19 July
John Rigby 21 June
John Stone 4 February
John the Baptist 24 June p 56
John Vianney 4 August
Jonah Prophet 21 September p 95
Joseph Cafasso 23 June 23
Joseph Cottolengo 30 April
Joseph Kentenich 15 September
Joseph of Arimathea 17 March
Joseph of Calasanz 25 August
Joseph of Copertino 18 September
Joseph of Nazareth 19 March p 30
Jude Thaddeus 28 October
Julia of Corsica 22 May p 48
Julian 12 February
Juliana of Norwich 13 May
Justin Martyr 1 June
Justina of Antioch 26 September

K

Katharine Drexel 3 March
Kenneth 11 October
Kentigern 13 January
Kevin 3 June
Kieran 9 September
Kilian 29 July

L

Laura Vicuna January 22
Laurence 10 August p 79
Laurence Giustiniani 8 January
Laurence of Brindisi 21 July
Laurence of Canterbury 2 February
Laurence O'Toole 14 November
Leo the Great 10 November
Leonard Murialdo 19 May
Leonard of Limoges 6 November p 115
Louis de Montfort 28 April
Louis IV 11 September
Louis IX 25 August p 86
Louis of Arnstein 25 October
Louis of Toulouse 19 August
Louise de Marillac 15 March
Lucy Brocadelli 15 November
Lucy Filippini 25 March
Lucy of Syracuse 13 December p 126
Luke Belludi 17 February
Luke Kirby 30 May
Luke the Evangelist 18 October p 111

M

Malachy 3 November
Margaret Clitherow 30 August
Margaret Mary Alacoque 16 October
Margaret of Antioch 20 July p 65
Margaret of Savoy 23 November
Margaret of Scotland 16 November
Margaret Ward 30 August

Maria Goretti 6 July
Mark Evangelist 25 April p 37
Mark of Aviano 13 August
Mark Stephan Crisinus 7 September
Martha 29 July
Martin I 16 September
Martin Lumberas 11 December
Martin of Braga 20 March
Martin of Porres 3 November
Martin of Tours 11 November p 116
Mary Anna of Jesus 26 May
Mary Dominica Mazzarello 13 May
Mary Magdalene 22 July p 68
Mary Magdalene dei Pazzi 25 May
Mary Mother of Jesus 8 September p 88
Mary of Egypt 2 April
Mary Poussepin 24 January
Mary Ward 30 January
Matilda 14 March
Matthew Evangelist 21 September p 94
Matthias 24 February p 24
Maura 2 November
Maximilian Kolbe 14 August p 82
Maximilian of Lorch 12 October
Mechthild of Magdeburg 15 August
Melchior 6 January p 10
Methodius 14 February p 22
Michael Archangel 29 September p 100
Michael de Sanctis 10 April
Michael Ghebre 28 August
Michael Rua 29 October
Monica Mother of Augustine 27 August

N

Nicholas I 13 November
Nicholas of Myra 6 December p 124
Nicholas of Tolentino 10 September
Nicholas Owen 22 March
Nicholas Palea 11 February
Nicholas Rusca 25 August
Nicholas Tavelić 14 November
Ninian 16 September
Norbert 6 June

O

Oliver Plunket 1 July
Oscar 3 February
Otto of Bamberg 30 June
Owen 4 March

P

Pancras 12 May
Paschal Baylon 17 May
Patrick 17 March p 28
Paul Apostle 29 June p 59
Paul Miki and Companions 6 February
Paul of the Cross 19 October
Paula 26 January
Paulinus of York 10 October
Peter Apostle 29 June p 58
Peter Canisius 21 December
Peter Chrysologus 30 July
Peter Claver 9 September
Peter Damian 23 February
Peter Faber 1 August
Peter Fourier 9 December
Peter Martyr 6 April
Peter Nolasco 25 December
Peter of Canterbury 6 January
Philip 3 May p 40
Philip Howard 19 October
Philip Minh 3 July
Philip Neri 26 May p 49
Pius V 30 April
Pius X 21 August
Priscilla 8 July

R

Ralph Crockett 1 October
Raphael Archangel 29 September p 102
Raphael Chylinsky 2 December
Raymond of Penyafort 7 January
Renata of Bayern 22 May
Richard of Chichester 16 June
Rita of Cascia 22 May p 47
Robert Bellarmine 17 September p 90
Robert of Chaise-Dieu 17 April

Robert of Molesme 29 April
Robert of Sala 18 July
Rose of Lima 23 August
Rose of Viterbo 6 March
Rupert 24 September
Rupert Mayer 3 November

S

Sabina 29 August
Sarah 9 October p 107
Scholastica 10 February
Sebastian 20 January p 12
Sebastian Kimura 10 September
Sebastian Valfré 30 January
Severinus 8 January
Sigismund 2 May
Simon de Rojas 28 September
Simon Fidati 2 February
Simon of Lipnica 18 July
Simon of Todi 20 April
Simon Stock 16 May
Simon the Zealot 28 October p 113
Sophie of Rome 15 May p 43
Stanislaus Kostka 18 September p 92
Stanislaus of Cracow 11 April
Stephen First Martyr 26 December p 127
Stephen Harding 16 July
Stephen I 2 August
Stephen of Grandmont 8 February
Stephen of Hungary 16 August
Stephen Pongrácz 8 September
Susanna 19 December
Sylvester Guzzolini 26 November
Sylvester I 31 December p 130
Sylvester of Chálon-sur-Saóne 20 November

T

Mother Teresa 5 September
Teresa of Ávila 15 October p 110
Theodore of Canterbury 19 September
Theresa of Portugal 20 June
Therese of Lisieux 1 October p 103
Thomas Aquinas 28 January

Thomas Becket 29 December
Thomas More 22 June
Thomas the Apostle 3 July p 60
Timothy 26 January p 14
Titus 26 January
Tobias 13 September

U

Ulric of Augsburg 4 July p 61
Ulrich of Zell 14 July
Ursula Haider 20 January
Ursula of Cologne 21 October p 112

V

Valentine of Rätien 7 January
Valentine of Terni 14 February p 21
Valentine of Viterbo 3 November
Veronica 4 February p 19
Veronica Giuliani 9 July
Veronica of Binasco 13 January
Vincent de Paul 27 September p 97
Vincent Ferrer 5 April
Vincent of Saragossa 22 January
Vincent Palotti 22 January
Virgil 24 September
Vitus 15 June

W

Walburga 25 February
Wenceslaus 28 September p 98
Wendelin 20 October
Willibrord 6 December
Wolfgang of Regensburg 31 October

My Name

My Name	Saint's Name	Page
A		
Adalbert	Adalbert	35
Agnes	Agnes	13
Agnesa	Agnes	13
Agostino	Augustine	87
Alastair	Alexander	41
Albert	Adalbert	35
Alec	Alexander	41
Alessandro	Alexander	41
Alex	Alexander	41
Alexander	Alexander	41
Alexandre	Alexander	41
Alexis	Alexander	41
Alexius	Alexander	41
Alice	Elizabeth	118
Alina	Mary Magdalene	68
Alison	Elizabeth	118
Andi	Andrew	121
André	Andrew	121
Andrea	Andrew	121
Andrew	Andrew	121
Anette	Anna	74
Angel	Angela Merici	15
Angela	Angela Merici	15
Angelica	Angela Merici	15
Angelina	Angela Merici	15
Angelique	Angela Merici	15
Angelo	Angela Merici	15
Angie	Angela Merici	15
Anika	Anna	74
Anita	Anna	74
Ann	Anna	74
Anna	Anna	74
Anne	Anna	74
Annette	Anna	74
Annika	Anna	74
Anthony	Anthony	54
Anton	Anthony	54
Antonio	Anthony	54
Antony	Anthony	54
Augustin	Augustine	87
Augustine	Augustine	87
Augustus	Augustine	87
Austin	Augustine	87

My Name	Saint's Name	Page
B		
Babette	Elizabeth	118
Babette	Barbara	123
Baltasar	Baltasar	10
Balthazar	Baltasar	10
Barbara	Barbara	123
Barney	Bernard of Clairvaux	84
Bartel	Bartholomew	85
Bartholomew	Bartholomew	85
Bastin	Sebastian	12
Bella	Elizabeth	118
Ben	Benjamin	32
Benedict	Benedict	62
Benjamin	Benjamin	32
Bennie	Benjamin	32
Benno	Bernard of Clairvaux	84
Benny	Benjamin	32
Beppe	Joseph	30
Berenice	Veronica	19
Bernadette	Bernadette	33
Bernard	Bernard of Clairvaux	84
Bernarde	Bernadette	33
Bernardine	Bernadette	33
Berney	Bernard of Clairvaux	84
Bernice	Veronica	19
Bernie	Bernard of Clairvaux	84
Bert	Robert Bellarmine	90
Betina	Elizabeth	118
Bettina	Elizabeth	118
Betty	Elizabeth	118
Blaise	Blaise	18
Blaze	Blaise	18
Bliss	Blaise	18
Bob	Robert Bellarmine	90
Boniface	Boniface	52
Bonus	Boniface	52
Brid	Bridget of Sweden	70
Briddy	Bridget of Sweden	70
Bridget	Bridget of Sweden	70

137

My Name	Saint's Name	Page	My Name	Saint's Name	Page

C

Carlos	Charles	114	Denys	Dennis of Paris	108
Casimir	Casimir	25	Diego	James	40
Casper	Caspar	10	Domenico	Dominic	78
Caterina	Catherine	38	Dominic	Dominic	78
Catherine	Catherine	38	Dominique	Dominic	78
Cécile	Cecilia	120	Dora	Dorothy	20
Cecilia	Cecilia	120	Dora	Dorothy	20
Charles	Charles	114	Doreen	Dorothy	20
Chiara	Clare of Assisi	80	Dorina	Dorothy	20
Chris	Christine	72	Dorinda	Dorothy	20
Christel	Christine	72	Doris	Dorothy	20
Christine	Christine	72	Dorothea	Dorothy	20
Chris	Christopher	71	Dorothy	Dorothy	20
Christopher	Christopher	71			
Claire	Clare of Assisi	80			
Clare	Clare of Assisi	80			

E

Colin	Nicholas	124	Elizabeth	Elizabeth	118
Connie	Conrad	34	Ella	Elizabeth	118
Conny	Conrad	34	Elsa	Elizabeth	118
Conrad	Conrad	34	Elsbeth	Elizabeth	118
Cosmas	Cosmas	96	Enrico	Henry	64
Cristina	Christine	72	Eoin	John	16
Cunegundes	Cunegundes	64	Ethelbert	Adalbert	35
Cyril	Cyril	22	Evan	John	16, 26, 44, 56, 128

D

F

Damian	Damien	96	Faustina	Faustina	106
Damien	Damien	96	Felice	Felix	46
Dan	Daniel	66	Felipe	Philip	40
Daniel	Daniel	66	Felix	Felix	46
Danny	Daniel	66	Flo	Florian	42
Dave	David	129	Florian	Florian	42
David	David	129	Franc	Francis of Assisi	104
Davide	David	129	Frances	Frances	27
Denis	Dennis of Paris	108	Francesca	Frances	27
Dennis	Dennis of Paris	108	Francesco	Francis of Assisi	104, 122

My Name	Saint's Name	Page
Francis	Francis of Assisi	104, 122
Francisca	Frances	27
Francisco	Francis of Assisi	104, 122
Francois	Francis of Assisi	104, 122
Francoise	Frances	27
Frans	Francis of Assisi	104, 122
Frantz	Francis of Assisi	104, 122

G

My Name	Saint's Name	Page
Gabriele	Gabriel	101
George	George	36
Gianni	John	16, 26, 44, 56, 128
Gillian	Julia	48
Gino	Louis	86
Giovanni	John	16, 26, 44, 56, 128
Giuseppe	Joseph	30
Goran	George	36

H

My Name	Saint's Name	Page
Hamish	James	40, 74
Hanna	Joan	50, 74
Hannah	Joan	50
Harry	Henry	64
Heiko	Henry	64
Heinar	Henry	64
Heiner	Henry	64
Henri	Henry	64
Henrik	Henry	64
Henry	Henry	64
Henryk	Henry	64
Hidda	Hildegard	91
Hilda	Hildegard	91
Hilde	Hildegard	91
Hildegard	Hildegard	91
Hildegarda	Hildegard	91
Hilke	Hildegard	91
Hilla	Hildegard	91
Hinrich	Henry	64
Hinz	Henry	64
Hodge	Robert Bellarmine	90
Hynek	Ignatius of Loyola	76

I

My Name	Saint's Name	Page
Iaian	John	16, 26, 44, 56, 128
Ian	John	16, 26, 44, 56, 128
Ignatius	Ignatius of Loyola	76
Ina	Catherine	38
Inigo	Ignatius of Loyola	76
Isabel	Elizabeth	118
Isabella	Elizabeth	118
Isoep	Joseph	30
Ivan	John	16, 26, 44, 56, 128
Ivanna	Joan	16, 26, 44, 56, 128
Iwan	John	16, 26, 44, 56, 128

J

My Name	Saint's Name	Page
Jacob	James	40, 73
Jacques	James	40, 73
Jaime	James,	40, 73
James	James	40, 73
Jamie	James	40, 73
Jan	James	40, 56, 128
Jane	Joan	50
Janet	Joan	50
Janine	Joan	50
Jannis	John	16, 26, 44, 56, 128
Jasper	Caspar	10
Jean	John	16, 26, 44, 56, 128
Jeanne	Joan	50
Jeannette	Joan	50
Jenny	Joan	50
Jerzy	George	36
Jill	Julia	48
Jim	James	40, 73
Jimmie	James	40, 73
Jimmy	James	40, 73

My Name	Saint's Name	Page	My Name	Saint's Name	Page
\Jimmy	James the Great	40, 73	Kim	Joachim	74
Joachim	Joachim	74	Kitty	Catherine	38
Joan	Joan	50	Klarissa	Clare of Assisi	80
Joe	Joseph	30	Klas	Nicholas	124
Joey	Joseph	30	Klaus	Nicholas	124
Johann	John	16, 26, 44, 56, 128	Konrad	Conrad	34
John	John	16, 26, 44, 56, 128	Kort	Conrad	34
Jon	Jonah	95	Kristina	Christine	72
Jona	Jonah	95	Kristine	Christine	72
Jonah	Jonah	95	Kristof	Christine	72
Joseph	Joseph	30	Kristoffer	Christine	72
Josiah	Joseph	30	Kryil	Cyril	22
Josie	Joseph	30	Krystel	Christine	72
Juan	John	16, 26, 44, 56, 128	Kurt	Conrad	34
Jula	Julia	48			
Julia	Julia	48			
Juliana	Julia	48			
Juliane	Julia	48			
Julie	Julia	48			
Julienne	Julia	48			
Juliet	Julia	48			
Juliette	Julia	48			

K

L

My Name	Saint's Name	Page
Karel	Charles	114
Karen	Catherine	38
Karin	Catherine	38
Kasmir	Casimir	25
Kasper	Caspar	10
Kat	Catherine	38
Katalin	Catherine	38
Kate	Catherine	38
Katharine	Catherine	38
Kathleen	Catherine	38
Kati	Catherine	38
Katina	Catherine	38
Katrin	Catherine	38
Katty	Catherine	38
Kerrin	Catherine	38
Kersti	Christine	72

My Name	Saint's Name	Page
Laurence	Laurence	79
Laurens	Laurence	79
Len	Leonard	115
Lena	Mary Magdalene	68
Lenard	Leonard	115
Lenardo	Leonard	115
Leni	Mary Magdalene	68
Leo	Leonard	115
Leon	Leonard	115
Leonard	Leonard	115
Leonardo	Leonard	115
Lewis	Louis	86
Lisa	Elizabeth	118
Lisbeth	Elizabeth	118
Lise	Elizabeth	118
Liz	Elizabeth	118
Lois	Louis	86
Louis	Louis	86
Lucas	Luke	111
Lucca	Luke	111
Lucetta	Lucy	126
Luci	Lucy	126
Luciana	Lucy	126
Lucie	Lucy	126

My Name	Saint's Name	Page	My Name	Saint's Name	Page
Lucienne	Lucy	126	Martin	Martin of Tours	116
Lucille	Lucy	126	Mary	Mary	88
Lucina	Lucy	126	Mateo	Mathias	24
Lucy	Lucy	126	Mathe	Mathias	24
Ludovic	Louis	86	Mathew	Mathew	94
Ludvik	Louis	86	Mathias	Mathew	94
Luigi	Louis	86	Matt	Mathias	24
Luis	Louis	86	Matteo	Mathias	24
Luke	Luke	111	Matthew	Mathew	94
Lutz	Louis	86	Matthias	Mathias	24
			Maud	Mary Magdalene	68
			Maura	Mary	88
			Maureen	Mary	88
			Max	Maximilian Kolbe	82

M

My Name	Saint's Name	Page	My Name	Saint's Name	Page
Maddy	Mary Magdalene	68	Maxim	Maximilian Kolbe	82
Madeleine	Mary Magdalene	68	Maxime	Maximilian Kolbe	82
Madeline	Mary Magdalene	68	Maximilian	Maximilian Kolbe	82
Madge	Margaret	65	May	Mary	88
Mae	Mary	88	Meg	Margaret	65
Magda	Mary Magdalene	68	Melchior	Melchior	10
Magdalen	Mary Magdalene	68	Mertin	Martin of Tours	116
Magdalene	Mary Magdalene	68	Mia	Mary	88
Maggie	Margaret	65	Michael	Michael	100
Marc	Mark	37	Michele	Michael	100
Marcel	Mark	37	Mick	Michael	100
Marcello	Mark	37	Mike	Michael	100
Marco	Mark	37	Miriam	Mary	88
Marcus	Mark	37			
Margaret	Margaret	65			
Margareta	Rita of Cascia	47			

N

My Name	Saint's Name	Page
Margarete	Rita of Cascia	47
Margarita	Margaret	65	Nancy	Anna	74
Margery	Margaret	65	Nesa	Agnes	13
Margot	Margaret	65	Netta	Anna	74
Mariana	Mary	88	Nicholas	Nicholas	124
Marie	Mary	88	Nick	Nicholas	124
Mariella	Mary	88	Nicky	Veronica	19, 124
Marilyn	Mary	88	Nicol	Nicholas	124
Marion	Mary	88	Nicolas	Nicholas	124
Marita	Mary	88	Nicole	Nicholas	124
Marjorie	Margaret	65	Nicolo	Nicholas	124
Mark	Mark	37	Nikolas	Nicholas	124
			Nina	Catherine	38, 72

My Name	Saint's Name	Page	My Name	Saint's Name	Page

P

Paddy	Patrick	28	Sheelah	Cecilia	120
Padraic	Patrick	28	Sheila	Cecilia	120
Padraig	Patrick	28	Sid	Dennis of Paris	108
Pat	Patrick	28	Sidney	Dennis of Paris	108
Patrick	Patrick	28	Simeon	Simeon	113
Patty	Patrick	28	Simeone	Simeon	113
Paul	Paul	58	Sissy	Elizabeth	118
Peggy	Margaret	65	Sofia	Sophie	43
Pete	Peter	58	Sofie	Sophie	43
Peter	Peter	58	Sonya	Sophie	43
Phil	Philip	49	Sophia	Sophie	43
Philip	Philip	40	Sophie	Sophie	43
Philipp	Philip	49	Stan	Stanislaus	92
Piotre	Peter	58	Stanislaus	Stanislaus	92
			Stefan	Stephan	127
			Stéphane	Stephan	127

R

			Steve	Stephan	127
			Steven	Stephan	127
Raphael	Raphael	102	Stevie	Stephan	127
Rick	Patrick	28	Sylvester	Sylvester	130
Ricky	Patrick	28			
Rita	Rita of Cascia	4765			
Robert	Robert Bellarmine	90			

T

Robin	Robert Bellarmine	90			
Ronnie	Veronica	19	Taffy	David	129
Rupert	Robert Bellarmine	90	Teresa	Theresa	103, 110
			Tess	Theresa	103, 110
			Tessa	Theresa	103, 110
			Theresa	Thérèse of Lisieux	103, 110
			Therese	Theresa of Avila	103, 110

S

Sally	Sarah	107
Sandy	Alexander	41
Sarah	Sarah	107

U

Seain	John	16, 26, 44, 56, 128			
Seamus	James	40	Ulla	Ursula	112
Sean	John	16, 26, 44, 56, 128	Ullrich	Ulric	61
Sebastian	Sebastian	12	Ulric	Ulric	61
Shamus	James	40	Ulrik	Ulric	61
Shane	John	16, 26, 44, 56, 128	Ursa	Ursula	112
Shawn	John	16, 26, 44, 56, 128	Ursina	Ursula	112
Sheamus	James	40	Ursola	Ursula	112
Sheela	Cecilia	120	Ursula	Ursula	112

My Name	Saint's Name	Page
Ursule	Ursula	112
Ursulina	Ursula	112

V

Val	Valentine	21
Valentino	Valentine	21
Vera	Veronica	19
Veronia	Veronica	19
Veronica	Veronica	19
Véronique	Veronica	19
Vicente	Vincent de Paul	97
Vincent	Vincent de Paul	97
Vincenz	Vincent de Paul	97
Vincenzo	Vincent de Paul	97
Vinz	Vincent de Paul	97
Vinzent	Vincent de Paul	97

W

Wazlaw	Wencelaus	98
Wencelaus	Wencelaus	98
Wenzeslaus	Wencelaus	98

X

Xavier	Francis Xavier	122

Z

Zane	John	16, 26, 44, 56, 128
Zara	Sarah	107

Vera Schauber and Michael Schindler have already published
several popular standard works on the Saints.

Martina Spinková is a painter, graphic artist and successful illustrator of children's books.

Kathleen Pearce is the author of several children's books published by
Don Bosco Publications.

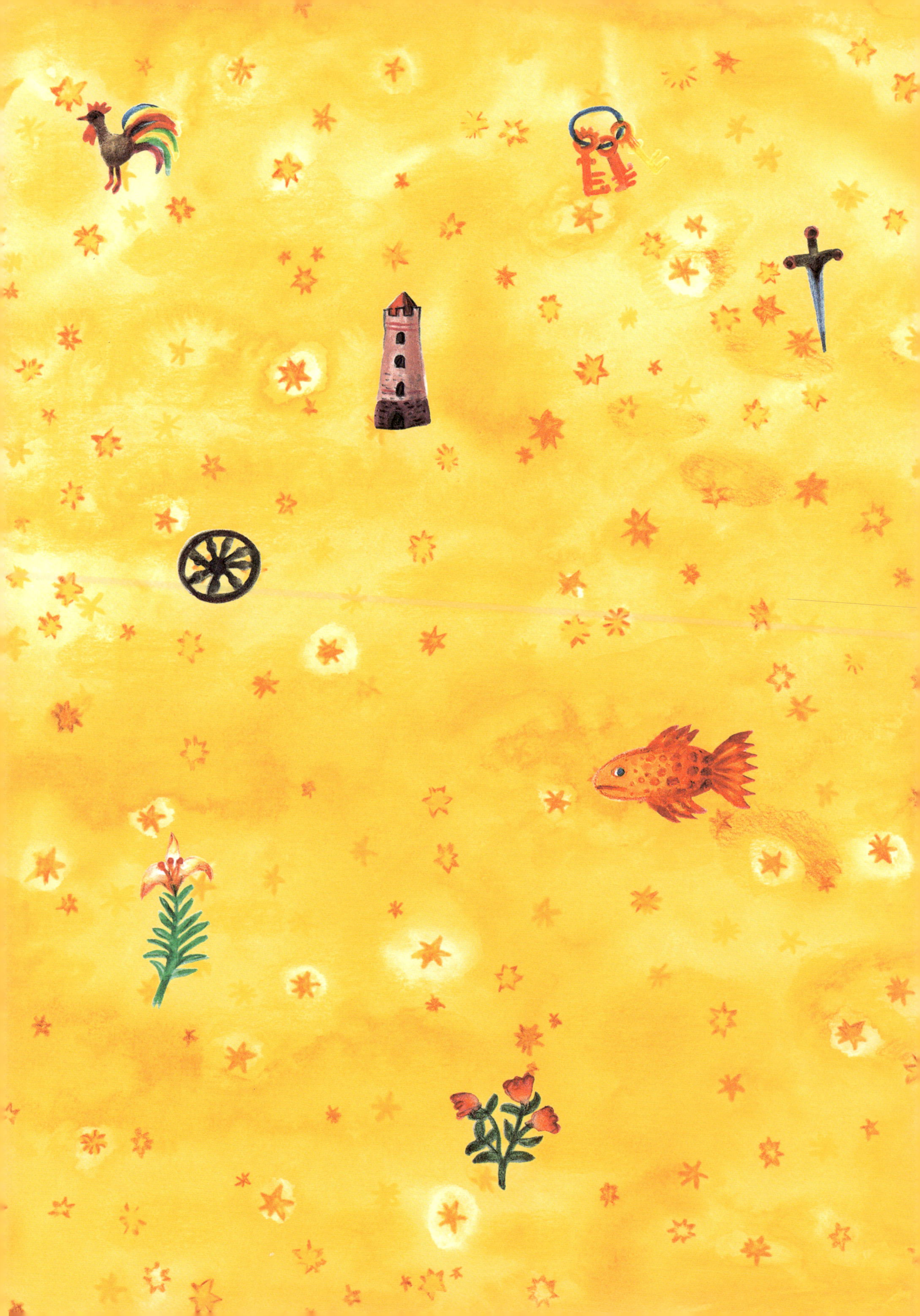